Challenges to Identifying and Managing Intangible Cultural Heritage in Mauritius, Zanzibar and Seychelles

Author

Rosabelle Boswell is a Senior Lecturer in the Anthropology Department at Rhodes University, South Africa and a Specialist of the Southwest Indian Ocean islands. Her research interests include ethnicity, heritage, gender and development. Boswell's PhD was on poverty and identity among Creoles in Mauritius and her most recent work is on the role of scent and fragrances in the heritage of the Swahili Islands of the Indian Ocean Region.

Challenges to Identifying and Managing Intangible Cultural Heritage in Mauritius, Zanzibar and Seychelles

Rosabelle Boswell

Monograph Series

The CODESRIA Monograph Series is published to stimulate debate, comments, and further research on the subjects covered. The Series will serve as a forum for works based on the findings of original research, which however are too long for academic journals but not long enough to be published as books, and which deserve to be accessible to the research community in Africa and elsewhere. Such works may be case studies, theoretical debates or both, but they incorporate significant findings, analyses, and critical evaluations of the current literature on the subjects in question.

© Council for the Development of Social Science Research in Africa, 2008
Avenue Cheikh Anta Diop Angle Canal IV, BP 3304 Dakar, 18524 Senegal
www.codesria.org
All rights reserved

Layout by Hadijatou Sy
Printed by Imprimerie Graphiplus, Dakar, Senegal

CODESRIA Monograph Series
ISBN: 2-86978-215-2
ISBN 13: 97828678-215-0

CODESRIA would like to express its gratitude to the Swedish International Development Cooperation Agency (SIDA/SAREC), the International Development Research Centre (IDRC), Ford Foundation, MacArthur Foundation, Carnegie Corporation, NORAD, the Danish Agency for International Development (DANIDA), the French Ministry of Cooperation, the United Nations Development Programme (UNDP), the Netherlands Ministry of Foreign Affairs, Rockefeller Foundation, FINIDA, CIDA, IIEP/ADEA, OECD, OXFAM America, UNICEF and the Government of Senegal for supporting its research, training and publication programmes.

Dedication

To my long lost ancestors and the heritages
they could have passed on to me.

Contents

Author 2
Dedication 5
Acknowledgements 8
List of Abbreviations 9
1. Introduction 11
2. Managing Heritage in Africa 17
3. The Indian Ocean Region 24
4. Theoretical Orientations 34
5. Image and Commerce: Mauritius 41
6. Violence and Compromise: Zanzibar 55
7. Socialism and Change: Seychelles 71
8. Conclusions 81
Notes 84
Bibliography 87

Acknowledgements

The following book would not have been possible without the assistance of numerous individuals and organisations. The initial research project was funded by the Council for the Development of Social Science Research in Africa (CODESRIA) via an Advanced Research Grant. I thank CODESRIA, the people of Mauritius, Zanzibar and the Seychelles for their kind participation in this research project. Much gratitude is due to the Nelson Mandela Centre for African Culture (NMCAC, Mauritius), the National Heritage Trust (Mauritius), the organisers of the Zanzibar International Film Festival (ZIFF) in 2004 and the National Heritage Division (NHD) in Seychelles.

List of Abbreviations

BIOT	British Indian Ocean Territory
CCM	Cham Cha Mapinduzi (Zanzibar)
CIDP	Chamarel Integrated Development Project (Mauritius)
COMESA	Common Market for Eastern and Southern Africa
CUF	Civic United Front (Zanzibar)
EAC	East African Community
ICH	Intangible Cultural Heritage
IOR	Indian Ocean Region
IOR–ARC	Indian Ocean Rims Association for Regional Cooperation
MMKA	Muvman Morisyen Kreol Afrikain (Movement for Black Mauritian Creoles)
MPL	Mouvement Pour Le Progrés (Movement for Progress, Mauritius)
MWF	Mauritius Wildlife Fund
NHD	National Heritage Division (Seychelles)
NHF	National Heritage Foundation (Mauritius)
NMCAC	Nelson Mandela Centre for African Culture (Mauritius)
OF	Organisation Fraternel
ROC	Rassemblement Organisations Creoles (Union of Creole Organisations)
SADC	Southern African Development Community
SDP	Seychelles Democratic Party
SenPA	Seychelles Small Enterprise Promotion Agency
SPPF	Seychelles Peoples Progressive Front
SPUP	Seychelles Peoples United Party
UNESCO	United Nations Education and Scientific Council
WHL	World Heritage List
YES	Young Enterprise Scheme (Seychelles)
ZIFF	Zanzibar International Film Festival

Map of Zanzibar Showing Some Villages and Stone Town

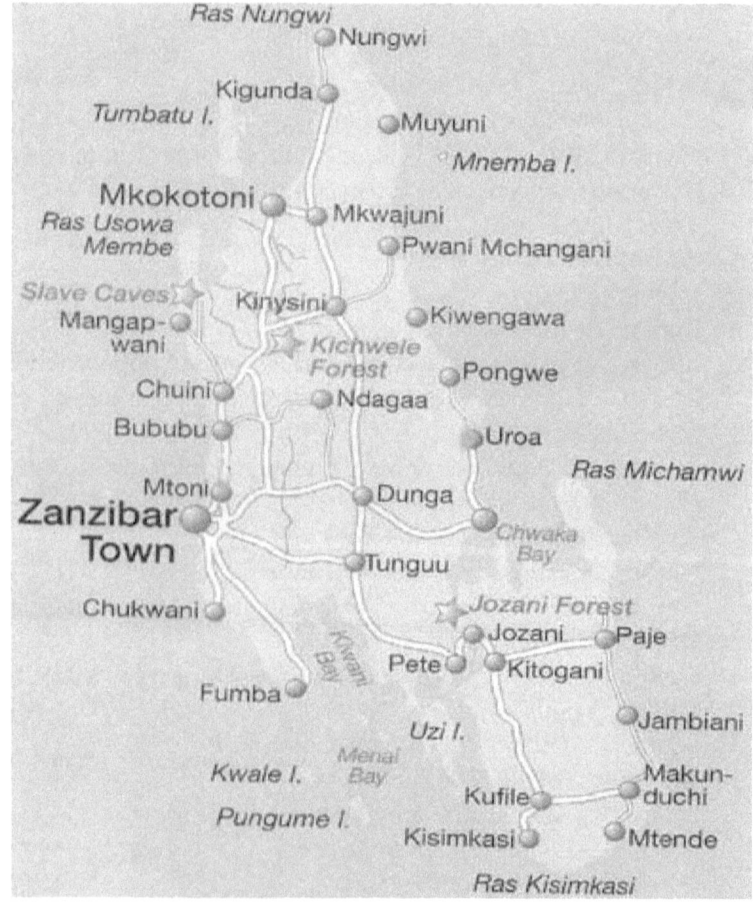

Source: www.zanzibari.net

1. Introduction

> Heritage is our legacy from the past, what we live with today and what we pass on to future generations.
>
> *World Heritage Information Kit*, Paris: UNESCO.

Heritage according to UNESCO 'is our legacy from the past.' It is also defined as irreplaceable 'points of reference' and, 'our identity'. While this statement is certainly true for certain peoples of Africa, it is not necessarily an accurate definition of heritage for all. This study argues that African scholars need to critically discuss the concept of heritage and reflect on the processes involved in its identification before accepting UNESCO's statement that heritage is a critical reference point for a cultural group or a fundamental aspect of one's identity. The study also offers some important critiques of heritage preservation, as advised by UNESCO. I argue that the mega-diversity of Africa and its neighbouring islands produce specific regional, historical and political factors, which influence the conceptualisation, nature and experience of heritage. It is therefore problematic for African leaders and leaders in the islands of Mauritius, Zanzibar and Seychelles wholeheartedly and uncritically to accept the discourses, means and approaches to heritage promoted by UNESCO and other significant heritage organisations.

UNESCO

UNESCO states that its initial interest in the preservation of heritage came after the destruction of archaeological sites and the theft of culturally precious objects during World War Two (see www.unesco.org). Since then, the organisation has resolved to become involved in protecting cultural artefacts and sites and in negotiating the effects of globalisation on indigenous practices and products. The organisation's normative/standard-setting instrument for the management of heritage and the creation of a World Heritage List (WHL), place UNESCO at the forefront of efforts to identify and preserve heritage. Further efforts by the organisation to enact protective legislation, impose penalties and to conduct awareness campaigns regarding heritage preservation (Edson 2004), also portrays the organisation as an entity in 'charge' of these matters. To a certain extent, it also suggests that heritage is an entity that is identified, managed and theorised in the West. As the studies in this text show, worldwide UNESCO attempts to control the process of heritage identification and management but finds it difficult to achieve this goal. At best, it remains a standard-setting entity that struggles to understand and to deal with the subjective expressions of heritage.

At the UNESCO General Conference in Paris in October 2003, the 120 members voted unanimously for a new international convention that would distinguish between tangible and Intangible Cultural Heritage (ICH). This dichotomisation was meant to indicate awareness of and means to approach ICH management. In 2004, there were already several worried comments (See various articles in *Museum International*, 2004.) about how difficult it would be to capture, safeguard and preserve intangible heritage.

In 'Indian Ocean Africa' (Alpers 2002), heritage is diversely conceptualised, experienced and made significant in daily living. This should compel scholars of heritage studies in the region to question received wisdom about heritage and its management. What discourses and practical frameworks are we using in identifying and dealing with heritage? Is the recent interest in heritage largely due to the international efforts of heritage regimes such as UNESCO, who have devoted an entire decade (2000-2010) to international discussions, projects and plans for the safeguarding and careful management of heritage? Or, is there an independent, politically motivated interest in questioning and identifying heritage in the new millennium?

This study was initially inspired by my earlier research on hybrid identities and the cultural and political marginalisation of hybrids (Creoles) in Mauritius. I began to ask why there was currently such a deep interest in heritage and heritage management. Given my work on Creoles, I also began to reflect upon whether alternative systems of thought (not necessarily culturally bounded), modes of living, symbolic expressions exist in hybridised contexts which disrupt currently dominant (and often negative) discourses about the African Diaspora in the Indian Ocean. I wondered how the African Diaspora societies under question, maintained alternative modes of being or fashioned new, hybrid cultures in their efforts to negotiate the burden of colonisation.

The findings presented here show that in the Indian Ocean region, there are potent, alternative knowledge foundations and experiences which continue to diversify social existence and livelihoods. These studies are vital not only for deeper insight into political structure and power relations but also necessary for the identification of alternative visions for sustainable development in Africa. Keeping these concerns in mind, this project focuses on challenges to identifying and managing cultural heritage in the Indian Ocean islands of the Seychelles, Mauritius and Zanzibar.

In the introduction, I identify key issues influencing heritage and its management in Africa. What have African heritage managers and institutions been concerned with thus far? What are their priorities and why? These first questions lead me to reflect on contemporary conceptualisations of heritage. Is there a singular definition for heritage? How has heritage been theorised in the West, where a dominant discourse about heritage has recently emerged?

This discussion is followed by an introduction to the Indian Ocean region. Here I argue that Zanzibar, Mauritius and Seychelles are multicultural and hybridised nations whose identities and heritage are influenced by a long history of trade, cultural exchange and domination. The islands are also part of region that has historical experience of non-western forms of globalisation. Specifically, they have experienced Indian, Indonesian and Middle Eastern cultural impacts. What forms of heritage, experiences of heritage and subsequently, forms of heritage management will such contexts yield? I end the section by stating that these islands are embedded in a modern, globalised economy — briefly explaining how these new dynamics may influence considerations of heritage.

These considerations lead to my hypothesis. The colonisation of Mauritius and Seychelles (which were both *terra nullius* at the time of slavery and colonisation), has in the first instance produced societies deeply affected by violence and subordination. This legacy is evident in both societies, as they struggle to assert their independence from former colonial powers and demand their right to determine which heritage matters to them. Secondly, the islands are profoundly hybridised spaces, where a long history of colonisation and settlement has produced creolised cultures. As I argue in the presentation of the hypothesis, the latter was a historically important means for social and physical survival. It is this creolisation that continues to influence heritage in Zanzibar, Mauritius and Seychelles — thus far, very few cultural managers are taking creolisation seriously in their approaches to heritage management. The fact of creolisation and the lack of 'hard' cultural boundaries mean that a sufficiently flexible and imaginative approach to the management of heritage is required in the region.

The overview of the Indian Ocean region is followed by the presentation of ethnography on Mauritius, Zanzibar and Seychelles. Documenting my anthropological fieldwork in these island societies, I discuss the historical and present influences of various social forces on intangible heritage. I also indicate the ways in which these forces have produced unique epistemologies, modes of culture communication and politics. Reflecting on the broader politics of heritage, I discuss the historical prioritising of tangible heritage (such as historical monuments, archaeological sites and cultural artefacts) and the fundamental implications of this for intangible heritage in the societies researched. I reflect on the part played by heritage protection regimes in the foundation of local approaches to heritage management, showing the tension between the need for local institutions to retain their freedom and the pressure put upon them to conform to external standard setting requirements. In this section, I also explore some of the logistical constraints to identifying and preserving intangible heritage in the region and the implications of particular political views on heritage management.

Research Methods

The research on challenges to the management of ICH in the Indian Ocean region is ongoing. Questions and issues that have arisen thus far necessitated a consideration of various research methods and methodologies. The primary research methods used in fieldwork for this project were participant observation and detailed semi-structured interviews, methods particular to anthropology. I also relied on existing documentation, archival research and gathered oral histories—particularly in the case of Seychelles data. The snowball sampling technique was employed in the selection of interviewees. As the chapters show, using the ethnographic approach has facilitated a deep and emic understanding of social dynamics in these island societies. It is acknowledged however, that further research in the islands will be necessary for a more substantive understanding of heritage to emerge.

To this end, it is imperative for readers of this text to understand that further ethnographic data on the subject of heritage management in Zanzibar, Seychelles and Mauritius is forthcoming. In the interim, what is presented here raises broad questions about the implications of a differing 'management' ethos in heritage circles. Specifically, for some agencies involved in heritage management (such as UNESCO for instance), particular approaches and priorities are evident in the form of assistance that they provide. Training, organisational support, capacity building and the provision of information and the values underpinning these activities may not match the needs and values of countries receiving assistance. As I show in the chapter on Seychelles, top-down and prescriptive thinking and practice (or a preference for these approaches), does not advance the goal of sustainable development. More important, these practices do not question existing and dominant approaches to heritage management. The data presented here also show that the requirements of heritage 'regimes' may convince cultural managers to see participatory, democratic, 'bottom-up' approaches to heritage as impractical and may also encourage such managers to be inflexible in their approach to heritage management.

In the literature on heritage, a clear distinction is made between tangible and intangible cultural heritage (henceforth referred to as ICH). According to Bouchenaki (2003), tangible heritage includes monuments and archaeological sites, while intangible heritage covers a wide range of non-physical elements of culture. These may be music, tales, rituals, systems of folk knowledge, and epics. There is consensus among heritage scholars that these two broad spheres of heritage (tangible and intangible) are not mutually exclusive. In the following I have focused on intangible heritage as articulated via ethnomusicology, occupation diversity and symbolic interpretation. The data show that these are linked to and embedded in (and therefore not separate from), existing tangible heritages — mountains, buildings/towns and physical landscape.

Further research on intangible heritage in the Indian Ocean societies of Mauritius, Seychelles and Zanzibar is currently underway and will focus on emic expressions of heritage and on intermediaries in the heritage identification and inscription process. The latter include tourism officials, guides and receivers of tourists. Further interviews are also underway with culture 'managers' (at UNESCO offices in Mauritius, Seychelles and Tanzania) and stakeholders in these islands (such as The Aga Khan Trust for Culture, Stone Town Authority, ZIFF organisers in Zanzibar and National Heritage Foundation (NHF), Creole Culture Watch, and Nelson Mandela Centre for African Culture (NMCAC) in Mauritius. The research is also taking into account the importance of historical and current regional cooperation (through the Southern African Development Community (SADC), the Indian Ocean Rims Association for Regional Cooperation (IOR-ARC), the East African Community (EAC) and (COMESA) the Common Market for Eastern and Southern Africa) for addressing common challenges such as ICH management. A more holistic picture of how Mauritius, Zanzibar and Seychelles are connected in their entry into heritage-building politics is emerging.

Challenges to Research

There have been several important challenges to research. The fact of national elections in Tanzania in 2005 meant that there was increased social and political tension in Zanzibar. Another major factor influencing research in Seychelles and Mauritius in 2005 was the outbreak of Chikungunya, a particularly debilitating (although not necessarily fatal), mosquito-borne viral disease that is affecting Mauritius and Seychelles, having reached epidemic proportions in Reunion Island.

Time and gender issues have also presented obstacles to the research process. Working full-time, managing a family while conducting this project has meant that I have not been able to devote as much time to critical reflection and actual fieldwork as I would have liked to. Further challenges to research (conceptual, political and relational) are outlined in the ethnographic discussion following Chapters Two and Three.

2. Managing Heritage in Africa

On 16 November 1972, member states of the United Nations Education, Scientific and Cultural Organisation (UNESCO) adopted a convention to protect the World Cultural and Natural Heritage. Since then, UNESCO reports on heritage refer to the groundbreaking work of the organisation on heritage issues. This work has made what is in many instances a privately or differently experienced, highly malleable entity into a standardised, public commodity to be managed according to a set of institutional standards. Furthermore, the 'official' discussions on heritage also presume that those involved in heritage management 'are ... aware and concerned about their interdependence, even their mutual entanglement — and] perceive that being implicated with significant others has a special importance for their own consciousness' (Werbner 2002:2). This self and group awareness is taken for granted and is viewed as (one might argue), a means for successful heritage identification and management in Africa. Heritage will be important to Africans and members of the African Diaspora because it allows us to be aware of our cultural distinctiveness, which is vital for the achievement of a meaningful life. However, as this study shows, not only is heritage diversely articulated and experienced (therefore requiring, if at all, particular management approaches), subjective and collective expressions vary in Africa and its Diaspora, diversifying our points of reference and our interaction. Existing heritage discourses therefore, introduce another cultural repertoire in a context (Indian Ocean islands), where there are already multiple, disparate and accumulating cultural and political repertoires. This study reveals some of these contradictions and difficulties. The following chapter is organised as follows: first a broad discussion of issues influencing heritage in Africa, second a reflection on colonisation and fragmented identities and how these affect the preservation of heritage, and third, the logistical challenges Africans and Indian Ocean islanders experience when attempting to identify and manage heritage.

Factors Influencing Heritage in Africa

General discussions of heritage in Africa seem to suggest that heritage is becoming an important political, economic and cultural resource. This is happening in a context that is currently witnessing two contradictory cultural flows: super-diversification and homogenisation. To elaborate, the rapprochement of Western globalisation to 'indigenous' villages and communities is producing cultural and economic homogenisation (in these communities) on a scale previously unseen. On the other hand, the migrations of people from mostly poor countries to North America and Europe are producing super-diversity in states previously imagined as mono-cultural.

Coupled with these changes is the increasing commodification of culture. Tourism is fast becoming a source of investment for host countries, which receive foreign investment either directly through corporate sponsors or indirectly, through tourism and research. International tourists are in turn increasing the demand for cultural commodities. These become travel souvenirs and help to retain the memory of cultural encounters. The boom in international tourism is turning heritage into a valuable commodity. This appears to be the case in Mauritius where several additional sites have been identified (since the research was completed) and are being assessed for heritage tourism purposes. Such commodifications and deterritorialisations are also said to contribute to increased anxiety, social destabilisation and the intensification of identity politics. In such contexts of political and social uncertainty, heritage preservation is supposed to offer a positive[1] means of control. It is also meant to give Africans (and everyone else) that warm, fuzzy feeling. If we can look to the past and preserve memories of belonging and security, we are better able to face the uncertainties of the present. Heritage then becomes a sanctuary and heritage politics a 'safe' way of relating to the world. Essentially, no one can be faulted for expressing their cultural uniqueness in a world where such diversity is disappearing, or being threatened. A question that I ask in this study is, do Africans and in particular, Indian Ocean islanders experience this particular anxiety? If they do not, why are they still concerned with the preservation of heritage?

What I found is that much effort is being put into the nomination of heritage sites to the WHL and the identification of these not only for tourism purposes but also for nation building. These efforts show the incorporation of heritage in the discourse of nation building and the extent to which heritage is constructed and influenced by dominant discourses. In the islands, emic expressions of heritage across cultural boundaries are hybrid, inter-subjectively defined and locally specific. And it seems that everywhere, national governments are quickly appropriating heritage as a means to 'simplify' this social complexity and to introduce ideologically uncomplicated discourses of their own. The latter is particularly apparent in the Mauritius example presented further on.

Some of the most visible challenges to heritage identification and heritage in Africa and its Indian Ocean diaspora include: problems with outdated laws, insufficiently skilled personnel, poor infrastructure and local political crises. These persist and also affect the potential to identify and nominate heritage for the WHL or the list of Oral Masterpieces. The response of one Indian Ocean state (the Seychelles) documented here shows the extent to which African islands struggle to express their heritage in the face of considerable pressure to meet nationally and internationally dominant ideas about culture. A programme of exchange and education, which aims to build technical capacity in Africa by 2009 is currently underway to address the above-mentioned issues.

The issue of African response to UNESCO's standard-setting instruments, its definitions of heritage, and the organisation's arguments about the preservation, seems to be largely determined by access to resources to manage heritage. However, poverty in Africa and in parts of the Indian Ocean world means that many people are focusing on the daily struggle for physical survival. This involves strategic focus on basic needs: education, health and employment, which in turn means that leaders and 'ordinary' people are not specifically interested in the identification and preservation of what can be percived as esoteric heritage. At the time of writing there were no measures in place to document the intangible heritage of Zanzibar. The focus was (as I argue in the chapter on Zanzibar) on tangible heritage. This focus is largely because Zanzibar forms part of Tanzania, one of the poorest countries on the continent. Despite the tense political relationship with Zanzibar, government on mainland Tanzania has to deal with the broader issues of education, health and employment — factors that do not always include heritage.

Another issue is that, in the Indian Ocean, experiences have always included encounters with super-diversity, creolisation and change. The drive to 'preserve' that, which is culturally distinct or even exotic, may be impossible, and what is considered exotic in the West may be commonplace in Africa and its neighbouring islands. Why preserve something, which we do not consider distinctive or special? These issues show that the challenge of heritage management in Africa and the Indian Ocean islands are not just logistical.

Nevertheless, in postcolonial states, heritage is important. It has been identified as a profound source of memory. One cannot critically reflect on heritage identification and management without a consideration of the effects of colonisation on memory and dialogues about identity.

The 'Invisible' Effects of Colonisation: Fragmented Identities

The continued effects of colonisation, difficult to quantify, analyse or publicise, affect Africans and the African diaspora in different ways. One of the common and often 'invisible' outcomes of colonisation is the sense of deprivation felt by Africans. Deprivation of land, belief, community and identity among others has produced a deep sense of loss and rootlessness. The more resilient among us have sought to capitalise on existing difficulties — seeing advantages in being the Other, appropriating or subverting hegemonic ideologies to achieve new autonomy and resistance. For most however, the colonial fixation on identity urges us to continually question the foundations and authenticity of our selves. This 'loss' of identity means that our memories of the past cannot be comforting, rather, these are brutal and what is left of our heritage is embedded in ethnoscapes of violence. Such feelings and experiences are exacerbated by the global media's pervasively negative portrayals of Africa and its people. In such contexts, can comfort or catharsis be found in identifying and preserving heritage?

Another 'imperceptible' outcome of colonisation is the devaluation of Africa and its peoples. The absence of African sites and heritages on the WHL concerns African leaders. The absence not only says something about Africa's position in the global economy, it also says something negative about the global value of Africa and its cultural expressions. With regard to the first, African leaders want to improve the terms of their states' integration into the global economy because for about 200 years (and from the perspective of Africans), the continent has not been positively integrated into this economy. Having a site on the WHL symbolises that the goal of positive integration is being achieved. With regard to the valuation of Africa, having a site inscribed on the WHL or having ones ICH placed on the list of Oral Masterpieces is a way of achieving or reinstating positive value. But what value do Africans and members of the African diaspora in the Indian Ocean region place on the continent? With regard to the islands mentioned in this study, colonisation brought to these regimes of value and sets of cultural definitions. These diminished existing viable, culturally diverse and dialectical senses of self and instituted primordial and bounded identities. In the Indian Ocean islands of Mauritius and Seychelles, the 'invisible' effects of colonisation are stark: slave descendants, who have internalised the colonial discourses, feel the absence of 'roots' as they cannot access the varied cultural traditions of their ancestors. More than this absence, during colonisation, the means of communication and rituals of non-Europeans were denigrated, their bodies mistreated and their understanding of the world disregarded. So slaves and others like them lost more than their identities, they lost the rich and diverse possibilities that could have made them into self-affirming human beings.

The invisible effects of colonisation have had many practical outcomes. They have entrenched social and economic inequality. In many postcolonial states, particularly in sub-Saharan Africa, resources are still largely controlled by the descendants of Europeans. In Mauritius, it is the landowning French descendants who have played a pivotal role in defining culture and prestige, and it is still they who control the economy together with a growing Hindu bourgeoisie. In Seychelles, both the French and English colonisers defined the black population as uncultured and without identity. In both island societies, pigmentocracies persist, encouraging a high value to be placed on whiteness. In Zanzibar, the Omani rulers had a lasting impact on Zanzibari identity and sense of power. Those of Afro-Shirazi descent were looked down upon and (African) mainlanders often treated in a racist manner. However, as I show here, there are Others who deploy multiple strategies for survival, oscillating between primordial and discursive expressions of identity, negotiating the burden of colonisation in various and successful ways.

Reflecting on the process of identity destruction during European colonisation, the anthropologist, John Comaroff (2001) says that for colonisers, simplifying the cultural diversity encountered was necessary and convenient. Necessary and convenient because simplification was a means for enforcing nolonial rule. Simplification, also and as Terence Ranger argues, the 'reinvention of tradition', allowed officials to control Africans without the constant use of force. This, known as indirect rule, involved the selection of a traditional leader to act as a political (and economic) broker between the coloniser and the colonised. The simplification and in many instances, blatant disregard for African cultures had material and political consequences, disabling a large number from realising the possible benefits of a hybrid and complex identity and the potential of this for social and economic advancement.

This simplification has had long term consequences entrenching dominant perceptions of culture and identity. And, as Moodie (2005) argues, reversing or changing dominant perceptions of culture and identity will take a long time. Responding to this, various African and Asian scholars, from Césaire, Fanon, Senghor to Mudimbe, Mamdani, Bhabha, Gilroy and Hall (to name a few), indicate the complicated work required for change to occur. Many of these authors stress how difficult it is to bring about change, when those living in the post-colony have not acknowledged the fact of their colonisation. With regard to heritage, the scholarly works of the above suggest that the meaningful management of heritage in Africa will require more than updating heritage legislation or creating suitable conditions for heritage managers to work in. The entire premise of heritage identification, preservation and management needs to be reviewed. Afrocentric writing on culture in 'original' Africa often call for a return to 'roots', Africans must document and assess the original contexts of cultural production so that they might offer a counterpoint to constructions of culture and identity. This may require a sort of 'anti-racist racism' as Sartre stated in his discussion of negritude. In this study, I argue that cultural heritage managers and researchers will find it difficult to identify pristine cultural practices and heritages or even master narratives of heritage in the Indian Ocean. Heritage is the result of cultural interaction and in the postcolonial states of Mauritius, Seychelles and Zanzibar, and that cultural interaction involves experiences of slavery, colonisation, violence and the cultures of the colonisers.

A quick glance at UNESCO's heritage management reports (see Fekri 2003) would also suggest that African heritage managers are perpetually under pressure to meet the requirements of UNESCO's World Heritage Committee and that there is little, or no space for negotiating heritage identification and management. A closer look reveals an obsession with logistics and what I would argue are not substantive issues that will encourage heritage managers to radicalise perceptions of and orientations towards heritage.

Logistics and the Visible Effects of Colonisation

In the UNESCO *Periodic Report on Africa* (Fekri 2003: 13) for instance, it is noted that 'the management of the cultural and natural heritage of Africa ... is beset with problems ... cultural heritage management programmes in Africa have been concerned mainly with preservation and conservation of archaeological monuments primarily from a technical point of view. Heritage legislation in Africa is also out of date, 'principles enshrined in the World Heritage Convention are absent, and the notion of 'heritage' is missing, popular terminology being 'ancient monuments' 'relics' (*Periodic Report Africa* 2003:45). These statements do not indicate the deeper factors influencing heritage and its management. These would include: perceptions of Africa and its island states, the persistence of colonial ideologies in the identification of heritage, and the poor consideration of history and historical experience in the making of these island societies.

The thinking about heritage in Africa also appears to be heavily influenced by European theories and experiences of heritage management. Many of these sources fail to identify the influence of broader political inequality on heritage, discussing inequality as a local factor (see Rowlands 2002:145-58). Some, like Michael Turnpenny (2004) notice that cultural heritage 'act as ... vehicles for deeper meanings ... cultural sites, places and artefacts can ... be considered to be physical representations of perceptions of self, community and belonging and their associated cultural values' (Ibid: 288-9). While these reflections offer a critical discussion of cultural values, they stop short of saying that there are enduring political inequalities that affect heritage management.

In the 2002 Africa periodic reporting exercise, it was 'found that only 53% of countries benefited from regular financing to cover training, salaries and conservation measures.' (*Partners for Africa Provisional Programme* 16 July 2005). Institutional weaknesses are cited as the main cause of these problems. Forty percent of 'endangered' sites on the World Heritage List are also African. In some cases, these are sites that are in war zones, remote parts of the continent and in countries where authorities have not properly maintained the sites. One might however, also ask whether these sites are 'endangered' because outsiders view them as such. What influence does the external valuation of heritage have on the identification of 'endangered' sites? Are there other 'endangered' sites or masterpieces, which do not feature on WHL or the list of Oral (and other) Masterpieces because investors do not value/prioritise the same heritage as locals? And, are the sites on the endangered list there because Africans do not perceive those heritages as valuable? Further research is required on these important issues.

What concepts and discourses of heritage would these dynamic, hybridised and postcolonial social spaces yield? Assuming that there might be the transmission of both new and 'mixed' cultural forms and practices, what corresponding form (if any) of management should be adopted? There are many different forms of political leadership, religions, economic practices and cultural ideologies. In my view, this dynamic diversity has not been carefully considered in the establishment of heritage management plans for Africa. Ultimately, these challenges have important conceptual and practical implications.

3. The Indian Ocean Region

In his discussion of the Indian Ocean world, the historian Edward Alpers notes that this world encountered various traders and seafarers long before the arrival of Europeans. In fact, long before the rise of Islam, traders from the Harappa Civilisation (Alpers 2002: 2), transported goods in the northwest Indian Ocean. South Asians who were in the region around 1000 BCE followed these traders. Madagascar, the fourth largest island on the planet, saw the earliest arrival of people to the southwest region with the settlement of Austronesians on the island in 4 AD. In the fourteenth century we see the emergence of a largely Islamic world, which was, according to the account of the Moroccan traveller, Ibn Battuta, 'outward looking, interconnected and multiethnic' (Alpers 2002:4). The Mascarene Islands (Mauritius, Reunion and Rodrigues) uninhabited at the time of such economic activity, only received immigrants in the seventeenth and eighteenth centuries. The geographical location of the Mascarenes and rough seas of the southwest Indian Ocean meant that for a very long time, these islands remained isolated.

Despite early and detailed accounts of life and trade in the Indian Ocean, it is, as Alpers tells us, difficult 'to gain imaginative control of this vast oceanic world' (2002: 8). Moreover, early writers found it hard to convey 'the vastness and complexity of the Indian Ocean' (ibid), largely because of the region's varied peoples, history, cultures and environments. Nevertheless, various scholars attempted to identify the region's unifying elements. Writing in the twentieth century, James de Vere Allen (1980 cited in Alpers 2002:10), says that in the Indian Ocean as a whole: race, culture and religion (essentially the early predominance of Islam), serve to unify the region. However, this approach does not capture the super-diversity of the region. It is Kenneth McPherson's discussion of the IOR as series of overlapping cultural zones (1984 in Alpers 2002:11), influenced by maritime trade and cultural diffusion that is most interesting and pertinent to this study.

In the following chapter, I identify elements contributing to cultural diffusion within and the unification of the IOR. In brief, these are: the experience of maritime trade; slavery; colonisation; possession of African diaspora communities; experience of the influence of southeast Asia and creolisation. I argue that these factors produced societies subject to similar forms of oppression, culminating in similar identities and politics. This is an important finding for heritage scholars and managers. We need to ascertain how regional factors and the *longue durée* of history influence heritage and identity.

Zanzibar

Zanzibar consists of two islands (Pemba in the north and Unguja islands in the south) that are situated off the coast of Tanzania. It is a semi-autonomous state that currently forms a part of one of the poorest countries in the world.[2] Today the population of Tanzania stands at 30,608,769. Zanzibar has a population of 1 million. Currently, the largest ethnic groups on the mainland are the Sukuma and the Nyamwezi, each representing about a fifth of the country's population. Other groups include the Haya, Ngonde, Chagga, Gogo, Nyakyusa, Nyika, Ngoni, Yao, and Masai. More so in Zanzibar and to a lesser extent Dar-es-Salaam, we find people of Indian, Pakistani, and Goan origin, and small Arab and European communities. In terms of religion, Islam remains dominant, while Roman Catholicism is the largest Christian denomination of Tanzania, with some six million adherents. Swahili and English are the official languages of Tanzania, but a large population still uses the language of their ethnic group.[3]

Recent anthropological (Askew 2002 and Fair 2001) and historical (Sheriff 1987) research, describes Zanzibar not only as an exceptionally beautiful island but also as an important site for international trade and cultural exchange. It is an island, as Pearson (1985 in Alpers 2002) would argue, characterised by dislocation and hybridisation, not stasis and homogeneity. For more than 300 years, Zanzibar islands and communities along the east African coast have cultivated trade links with cities and people of Oman and the Persian Gulf. The more than 800 Arabic manuscripts[4] lodged at the Zanzibar National Archives offer proof of a well-established cultural and political connection between Asia and Africa before the arrival the Europeans in the region. The connection between the Asian settlements of Bombay (India), Shiraz (Persia), Muscat, Aden (Oman), Mombasa, Kilwa (east Africa) and Zanzibar was largely facilitated by the presence of the monsoon season that allowed traders and sailors from the east to encounter the Bantu and Cushitic people living along the African coast. On the southern tip of Zanzibar, the village of Shangani (Stone Town) a small fishing village in the twelfth century rapidly became a trading centre and *the* commercial empire of the Indian Ocean region. The town experienced occupation by the Portuguese, who arrived there in 1498 and were ousted by sultan Bin Seif of Oman 200 years later. Bin Seif built the magnificent *Ngome Kongwe* (Old Fort) to defend Stone Town and the wealth of the Omanis from the Portuguese and Mazrui Arabs based in Mombasa. For Zanzibar is favourably located for monsoon trade. Its deep and protected ports (that have coral reefs all around) and (its once) abundant source of timber and mild weather meant that it was ideally suited for trade, settlement and the cultivation of spices.[5] In the early nineteenth century, these factors ensured that Zanzibar became an important stopover and source of wealth for African, Persian and Omani travellers and settlers in the Indian Ocean. Today the physical remnants of this wealth can still be seen in Zanzibar.

The particularly flourishing trade in African slaves[6] until the end of the nineteenth century and the relocation of the Omani sultanate from Muscat to Zanzibar in 1832 provided these traders with a further impetus to move to the island and settle there. Writing about the prosperity of Zanzibar, Laura Fair notes that 'Slaves, and the profits derived from both their sale and their labor, were at the very heart of Zanzibar's transformation from a small and relatively unimportant Swahili town to the centre of a vast trading empire stretching from central Africa to halfway around the globe' (2001: 12). Slaves, mostly from east Africa, transformed the island into a complex, multicultural society and 'the most productive clove plantations in the world' (Fair 2001: 13). In 1897[7] slavery was abolished in Zanzibar. But clear distinctions remained between slaves and the free, urbanites and rural dwellers, mainlanders and islanders and Arab and African. Divisions that are still apparent in the pre- and post-revolution politics of Tanzania.[8]

In 1964 there was a revolution and there was the union of Tanganyika and Zanzibar to form Tanzania. This attempted to solidify identity, redistribute resources and simplify an otherwise complex and fluid social world into a homogeneous whole. This process was largely achieved through violence. 'In one night of terror, some 12,000 Indians and Arabs were massacred by the army and many of Stone Town's African inhabitants, promoting the mass exodus of all but one percent of Stone Town's non-Africans.'[9] For many, such violence was a means to 'reverse an earlier historical memory of violence against Africans' (Parkin 2001: 153).

Mauritius

In many ways, Mauritius is similar to Zanzibar. Mauritius too, has experienced slavery. It is still highly stratified and ethnically segregated. It also has a significant minority of slave descendants. In contemporary times, the Hindu majority of the island retains close cultural and political ties with India. Nevertheless, the island society is thoroughly creolised and globalised, the latter evident in the marketing of Mauritius as an international tourism destination, an offshore banking centre and most recently, a digital technology hub. What does this mean for heritage management in Mauritius? Essentially, it means that heritage in Mauritius will be influenced by the process of globalisation. However, Mauritius's history also tells us that there are deep historical factors that continue to influence identity and perceptions of heritage on the island. A brief look at this history is therefore necessary.

Mauritius lies almost 800 kilometres east the island of Madagascar, the nearest considerable land mass (Benedict 1965). It is an independent or sovereign state that currently dominates the economic landscape of the Mascarenes. Historically, Mauritian society came about with the arrival of slaves from Africa and India and immigrants from India, China and Europe. The Dutch were the first to arrive in 1598 and were supplanted by the French in 1710. Around this time (1718–1725), a small party of Frenchmen from the neighbouring island of Reunion, also attempted to settle Mauritius. Ten years later (1735) the French renamed the island *Ile de France* and captured slaves off the east coast of Africa and Madagascar to cut down the ebony forests, build roads, ports and houses, and plant sugarcane. After a series of heavy battles with the French, the English managed to wrest control of the island in 1810 and renamed it Mauritius.

Slaves were brought from Africa (particularly along the Swahili 'corridor' from Mozambique to Mogadishu and consisted of Makua, Ngindo, Yao and Ngoni) Madagascar and India (Pondicherry). Once in Mauritius, they were subject to French laws and restrictions. The *Code Noir* or 'Black Code' of 1723 (Sala-Molin 1987) for example, forbade marriage, sexual relationships between whites and blacks and severely impacted on slave dignity and independence.

With the abolition of slavery in 1835, the British set up an apprenticeship system which 'was designed to accustom ex-slaves ... to their new responsibilities as free citizens' (Teelock 2001: 212). Apprentices were neither slave nor free. They were forced to work for no pay and those who chose not to accept the six-year apprenticeship and were caught not working were arrested for vagrancy. At this time, nearly 450,000 people of Indian descent were also brought in from the sub-continent of India to work as indentured labourers on the island (Teelock 1998). According to Teelock (2001: 234) these labourers, known as Dhangars (or Hill Coolies) came from Chota Nagpur. These were a semi-aboriginal people who had come from the 'hills' to find work on the 'plains'. Labourers were also recruited from the United Provinces (i.e. Gonda, Benares and Ghazipur) and the Bihari Districts (Patna, Tirhoot and Bhagalpur). In the second half of the nineteenth century Gujerat Muslims arrived from Kutch and Kathiavad while Parsi Muslims arrived from the Surat district in India (Ibid p. 313). Most of the Chinese living in Mauritius at this time came from Kwan Tung and Fukien provinces and Canton in China (Ibid p. 315).

Creoles, primarily the descendants of Afro-Malagasy slaves (and some of mixed Chinese, African and European ancestry), make up 20 percent of the population. In 1972, the first government of Mauritius declared this group (including Franco-Mauritians) the General Population. This resulted in Creoles being associated with a residual group and being politically categorised as a people with no identity. But there is significant social and political variation within the Creole category. Those born in Mauritius are referred to as the *Kreol Morisyen* and other Creole groups living in Mauritius today (who contribute to the population's profile), originate from the Indian Ocean islands of Rodrigues (*Rodriguais*), Seychelles (*Seychellois*) and the Chagos Archipelago (*Ilois*). Each of these sub-categories has particular cultural and social practices that distinguish them within the Creole category. The Anglo/Franco-Mauritians and descendants of the Chinese make up the remaining percentage of the population. Today, there are four major religions and approximately 22 languages spoken in Mauritius. English and French are used for business purposes but it is *Kreol* (the dialect developed by the descendants of slaves and Indian indentured labourers) that is the *lingua franca*.

Today Mauritians number about 1.5 million people and they form part of a nation that lives in one of the most densely populated countries in the world, with 579 people per square kilometre. The island's Indian population (mostly adherents of Hinduism) dominates the ethnic landscape and constitute sixty percent of the total population, while Creoles, primarily the descendants of Afro-Malagasy slaves (and some of mixed Chinese, African and European ancestry), make up 20 percent. The Anglo/Franco-Mauritians and descendants of the Chinese make up the remaining percentage of the population. From the mid-1980s, the country made remarkable economic progress and a majority of Mauritians benefited from the island's good fortune. By the late 1990s, Mauritians in general expected the country to experience further industrialisation and some expressed their wishes for an end to ethnic division and discrimination.

Until the 1960s the white minority tended to dominate business and politics in Mauritius. But for the last 30 years, Mauritius has experienced a changing field of representation and power that has seen the empowerment of the Hindu majority. Significant economic growth from tourism, textile industries and foreign investments is bringing new kinds of social hierarchy, and possibilities for advancement in the form of class and supra-ethnic networks are emerging. However, being the descendants of immigrants and inheritors of colonial and caste values, Mauritians maintain a deep interest in 'roots' and purity, which they perceive as necessary for the achievement of belonging and as the source of order in their plural society. The latter has been particularly difficult for Creoles because knowledge of their origins is hazy and they have not been able to cultivate a 'roots' discourse. Furthermore, until the efforts of historians[10] in the twentieth century, the origins of these slaves were largely unwritten, making it difficult for them to articulate their identity or challenge portrayals of their values and practices. In my view then, for Creoles the only means of retaining 'roots' and safeguarding heritage (including a positive vision of themselves) has been through their oral tradition. Most recently (and as I document in the chapter on Mauritius), pro-Creole groups, historians and some Creoles have attempted to anchor their identity in heritage sites, so as to craft a tangible presence of their identity in the dominant (roots oriented) local identity discourse. Other ethnic groups are not exempt from similar action. As I write, various ethnic groups in Mauritius are active in identifying sites to be preserved as part of 'their' heritage. I predict that it will become difficult for heritage managers in Mauritius to critically reflect on identity (and heritage) construction. With regard to the Creoles, their marginalisation in Mauritian society means that opposition to 'bona fide' elevations of slave history and identity will be rejected or dismissed on grounds of racism or gross misunderstanding of the situation of Creoles. With regard to other, less marginalised groups, the state's emphasis on diversity preservation (in itself an oxymoron!) will compel the latter to entertain and follow through with calls to preserve heritage sites associated with the history of particular ethnic groups.

The question of how to objectively view heritage is a difficult one to answer. In the Indian Ocean islands of Zanzibar, Mauritius and Seychelles, how can managers objectively view and approach heritage without hardening identities and reinforcing group boundaries? Going back to McPherson's discussion of the region as a series of overlapping zones, subject to creolisation and globalisation, heritage preservation seems at odds with the level and speed of social and cultural development in the Indian Ocean. In the next section, I introduce the Seychelles islands and some of the factors influencing heritage in that archipelago, noting the same kind of super-diversity and efforts to suppress it.

Seychelles

Seychelles is a vast archipelago consisting of 115 granite islands and seventy widely scattered coral islands in the northwest Indian Ocean region that until

300 years ago remained uninhabited. The geographical isolation of these islands encouraged the evolution of diverse fauna and flora. The *Vallée de Mai* (declared a natural World Heritage Site by UNESCO in 1988), is a biodiverse forest situated on the westward island of Praslin. When explorers came across the forest in the eighteenth century they believed it to be the Garden of Eden. One species found in the forest, the *coco-de-mer*, has become part of world legend.

In the late eighteenth century the Seychelles became a dependency of Mauritius. In 1742, the governor of Mauritius, Mahé de Labourdonnais, sent a first exploratory mission to the islands to see if they were fit for settlement. The first inhabitants, twenty French families from Mauritius, arrived in 1770 and settled on the island of St-Anne. They brought slaves with them and hoped to produce viable plantations. Initially, the settlers attempted to cultivate sugar and then spices but soon discovered that the granite-laden soils of the island would not support these crops. The settlers were forced to turn to the islands' ready supply of coconut trees to make a living, and did so by using the various products of the trees to produce coconut oil, alcoholic drinks and fibres (for rope-making and weaving). Bad weather, pirates and the fluctuation of international markets regularly challenged these efforts, and income from the copra industry had to be further supplemented with the planting of vanilla, patchouli and other fragrant herbs for the international perfume market. In 1835 the ready supply of labour was challenged. Slavery was abolished in both the Seychelles and Mauritius. In that year, four thousand black Seychellois were released from the bondage of slavery. However, Seychelles remained under British rule even though it became a (British) colony separate from Mauritius in 1903. It was only in 1976 that the Seychellois managed to negotiate their independence from colonial rule. The British required that the two pro-liberation parties, the Seychelles Democratic Party (SDP) and the Seychelles Peoples United Party (SPUP), agree to share power, so as to represent the interests of both the existing land-owning elite and the masses. In return, the British government would allow the islands to become independent and the Seychellois would get to keep the islands of Aldabra and Farquhar, which until then the British controlled as part of the British Indian Ocean Territory (BIOT).

During those years, the descendants of slaves in the Seychelles developed many different skills, means of communication and social relationships. Recent accounts (Berge 1987) of life on the plantations indicate that it was a difficult existence. The society was racially segregated and the contributions of slaves (economic, social or cultural) were rarely, publicly acknowledged or respected. For instance, until independence in 1976, many existing plantation owners were 'paying' labourers with *arrack* (rum), continued to force their attention on female labourers, and expected them to live in appalling conditions.

Despite such hardships, slave descendants became economically efficient, planting their own gardens, fishing, hunting and weaving. Many also enriched their lives by participating in regular performances of the *moutia*:[11] dance, music and oratory performed at the beach side or in one's courtyard. The growing population, boosted mostly by slaves arriving from Madagascar, Zanzibar and Mauritius, contributed to particular cosmologies, ideas and practices in the Seychelles. Similarly, continued belief in *gris-gris* (black magic), efforts to maintain multiple livelihoods and similar music forms and a focus on oratory all suggest that significant cultural and social exchange occurred in slave communities. In the 1870s, the arrival of freed African slaves in Mahé added to the social complexity and diversity of the society. Because the Seychelles islands were so remote, they were also perceived as an ideal place of exile for 'important' individuals from the African continent.

A year after Seychelles achieved its independence from Britain, Albert Rene, a minister in the cabinet of the then president James Mancham, drew upon Tanzanian military assistance and staged a coup. Troops of soldiers landed on Seychellois soil, seized arms (including pirate cutlasses currently deemed 'heritage' by local inhabitants) and turned the government over to Rene and his new party — the Seychelles Peoples Progressive Front (SPPF). From 1977 to 1993, socialism ruled the country. Education camps were set up, privately owned estates or plantations were taken over by the government, private enterprise was discouraged and soft loans were offered to the population to assist them with accommodation, education and subsistence. Polish, Chinese, Soviet and Cuban partnerships were also established. Engineers, teachers and shipping experts from these countries came to the Seychelles to assist the local population in their transition from a plantation to industrial economy. During this time, the government sought to promote the archipelago as a prime tourist destination. Islets were leased[12] to international businessmen and other wealthy individuals. Hotels were built, particularly along the east coast of Mahé.

At the time, there was very little focus on the cultural riches of the island. The stories and contributions of the slave descendants did not feature much in the social and economic transformation of the island. The emphasis lay on the island's natural assets and tourism was geared to mostly white tourists in search of recreational pursuits. With these facts it could be argued then that the Seychellois were not actively responding to outsiders' 'imagination' of their nation and society. However, in terms of their resistance to colonial rule and in their conscious attempts to effect radical political change they were in fact engaging with powerful political perceptions of their nation and were making the effort to forge an independent society and identity.

Politics in Mauritius, Zanzibar and Seychelles

Mauritius remains a highly ethnicised society. In the 1980s and 1990s both identity and belonging became powerful themes in the interrogation of the position of Creoles in the society. Songs produced by Creole musicians and the stories told by elders focussed most vividly on Creole identity and belonging in Mauritian society. What I found in the course of research is that those ethnic groups 'certain' of their history and empowered to display their heritage participated in the rapid conquest of space on the island. This process reinforced ethnic segregation and emphasised separate origins. In the new millennium it is still being promoted by the tourism ministry (intent on maximising the number of cultural options available for tourist consumption), and inadvertently assisted by some revisionist historians such as Norbert Benoit and Jocelyn Chan-Low (who are concerned to articulate history that has previously been distorted or misrepresented), and religious leaders intent on maintaining or increasing their religious following. One such religious leader, Henri Souchon, was noted[13] for speaking about Mauritian cultures as fruits in the syrup of nationalism and that this ought not to be destroyed through hybridisation or 'jam' making.

My fieldwork revealed[14] that ethnic politics and segregation are also apparent in religious symbols and monuments that commonly appear in public space, such as on mountain slopes, main roads and in the sea. I argue that in many instances these also indicate the relative power of the ethnic group, sometimes discouraging others from accessing or enjoying the particular space that the icon or monument occupies. A good example of this is the sacred lake at the top of the island. Identified as a symbol of the Ganges and the centrepiece for the Hindu pilgrimage of *Maha Shivaratri*, it is distinctively for people of Hindu faith. While those of non-Hindu faith are not barred from visiting the place they are made to feel that they cannot make their own 'inscriptions' there. The pilgrimage to the sacred lake is also attracting more political and economic resources. Thousands of pilgrims gather at the site every year and this requires significant coordination on the part of municipalities, the fire department and health services. Furthermore, in the interest of non-sectarianism, government leaders are expected to attend the opening religious ceremonies and the level of attention paid to such cultural ceremonies highlights the importance of the ethnic group involved. At some ceremonies political attendants (such as Paul Berenger, the current Prime Minister of Mauritius) are encouraged to wear appropriate ethnic dress supposedly to indicate their lack of ethnic prejudice. To the broader public, this often appears as a show of political and ethnic allegiance.

A similar level of ethnic segregation is apparent in Zanzibar. There, significant divisions remain between those of Afro-Shirazi and Omani descent. Or at least, that these divisions are articulated in the island's politics. In the Seychelles, the establishment of a socialist government encouraged the hardening of Creole ethnic identity. Although the revolution had not failed the people of Seychelles in the material sense, (under the SPPF government, many poor families had received soft or un-obligated loans and welfare cheques that had enabled them to build or buy a home) it did encourage slave descendants to see themselves as belonging to a homogeneous social group. This was achieved by encouraging the Seychelloise to value their maternal tongue, Kreol. To this end, a language institute, *l'Institit Kreol*, was created for the study, documentation and development of the dialect. The use of Kreol in business, schools and in the media also helped to encourage a more favourable view of the dialect. However, it also fostered an image of Creole identity as unchanging, bounded and homogeneous. The socialist government also disallowed private enterprise, seeing this as a contributor to socio-economic inequality. As I show in the chapter on Seychelles, there is a history of multiple livelihoods among Creoles in Mahé and there is still deep interest in maintaining diverse or multiple occupations. What these tell us is that Creoles living there wish to express their diversity, creolisation and social flexibility.

In the ethnographic chapters following the theoretical orientation, it is argued that politics continues to influence heritage in these three island societies. Specifically, ethnic divisions and recent political change (socialism in Tanzania and Seychelles for example) are influencing the nature and extent of heritage management. In the concluding chapter on Seychelles, I come back to an important issue raised in the overview of heritage and heritage management in Africa — to what extent do external perceptions of and policies for Africa influence heritage management on the continent?

4. Theoretical Orientations

Reflecting on both tangible and intangible heritage, Bouchenaki (2003: 1) states that 'an anthropological approach to heritage leads us to consider it as a social ensemble of many different, complex and interdependent manifestations'. This complexity is evident in the Indian Ocean region, sites of rich oral history, music and customs. Viewed from afar, the islands of Zanzibar, Seychelles and Mauritius have particular political structures and geographies. However, a closer look reveals that they are inextricably linked by their common historical experience of maritime trade, slavery and creolisation. These aspects have to be considered when deciding on an appropriate theoretical framework for the study of heritage in the IOR. In the previous chapter, I referred to McPherson's idea of the IOR as overlapping cultural zones. From this perspective, regional identity is constructed on the relationship between maritime trade and cultural diffusion. McPherson's approach offers a useful base for reflections on the nature and management of heritage in the IOR, especially because it points to both diversity and unity in the region. Using this idea, I propose that these island societies are inextricably linked entities, with particular distinctive social facets that render each one unique. The fact of a long and common history, the production of similar social and cultural hierarchies, exposure (in current times) to similar influences of trade and globalisation, means that the inhabitants of Zanzibar, Mauritius and Seychelles share common historical experiences. Does shared experience produce similar social and cultural perspectives? Before attempting to answer this important question, one has to look at how the various macro-political experiences shaped the island societies researched.

In brief, exposure to maritime trade, slavery, colonisation and the specific geographic limitations of island life produced a largely hybridised space. Cultural interaction (forced and voluntary), compelled many islanders to encounter one another's customs, languages and perceptions of life, fuelling creolisation. Slavery and colonisation also produced a socially and politically oppressed or oppressive people, who in turn created racial and cultural hierarchies. Today, dominant groups in these island societies are intent on maintaining segregation, believing (as the Mauritius case shows), that cultural purity will enable them to meaningfully reconnect with their motherland and to display identity. These ideas are not solely the result of being 'abandoned' in unfamiliar lands. They are inspired by a long and varied history of resistance against cultural and racial mixing. Nevertheless, these societies, isolated from Africa and mainland Europe/ Asia, became hybridised, a process rejected by some but experienced by all. In my research, I found that hybridity has become central to personal existence and to cultural expression.

Thus the issue of hybridity is of great import to heritage and consequently, its management in the IOR. However, an overview of discussions and perceptions of heritage reveals an obsession with the presumed boundedness and homogeneity of heritages. In many instances, heritage is seen as a source of 'roots' or a means to establish belonging in a presumed, homogeneous landscape. Heritage scholars influenced by Western notions of the concept tend to state the imperativeness of identifying and safeguarding heritage. As an anthropologist working in Africa, this view is reminiscent of the time at which anthropologists romanticised the 'native', searched for the exotic at all costs and attempted to salvage elements of traditional culture. It seems that in the new millennium anxiety is at an all time high, as cultural boundaries melt away and all are subject to the uncertainties of a global market and society. In this context, Malthusian (or catastrophic) perceptions of social evolution encourage heritage bodies to romanticise the past and to 'protect' the integrity of existing heritage. Doing research in the IOR revealed that people's identity or sense of self may be defined by mobility, displacement and hybridity as much as it may be influenced by stability, homogeneity and 'roots'. In fact, in the IOR, the latter is an ideal while the former is a reality. What does this mean for heritage managers in the region? Drawing on Western models of heritage management and the conceptualisations of heritage that inhere in these models, heritage managers in the region are not able to fully encounter heritage in the IOR. The externally imposed models and standards for management cannot help them to articulate their country's heritage.

Nestor Garcìa Canclini's early critique of patrimony/heritage discusses dominant ('Western') thinking about heritage, which conceives of it as 'a gift of symbolic prestige that has to be preserved ... not discussed or analyzed' (1995: 108). Garcìa Canclini offers a political critique of heritage, seeing it as an unequally distributed and appropriated gift that is deemed to be 'authentic' but actually consisting of the constructed symbolic capital of the rich/powerful; their resource for reproducing difference between groups and for the reproduction of hegemony. Garcìa Canclini does not refer directly to broader political inequality, or the extent to which heritage regimes might reproduce difference and reinforce hegemony. Here I argue that the concept of heritage requires deconstruction and that to do this, one needs a politically radical consideration of history and heritage. This will enable heritage managers in Africa to consider the extent to which the adoption of contemporary heritage practices by local people reflects a conscious engagement with those values in terms of their own priorities and interests.

The values underlying the 'Western' management ethos and their openness to alternative interpretations of heritage are hinted at in the *UNESCO Universal Declaration on Cultural Diversity*. In Article 7 of the Declaration, intangible heritage is defined as: 'oral traditions, customs, languages, music, dance, rituals, festivities, games [and] culinary arts'. UNESCO perceives intangible cultural resources as a means to preserve human diversity (in the face of modernisation and Western globalisation) and to ensure sustainable development. The emphasis on preservation echoes global concern with the effects of homogenisation. The emphasis on preservation is at odds with the reality of super-diversity and ongoing creolisation in the Indian Ocean region. Moreover, it is impossible to ensure (or even achieve) sustainable development in a global society driven by the capitalist ethos. Perhaps the Declaration should be rephrased to say 'encourage encounters with human diversity'. However, this could be seen as a problem, because diversification (perceived among liberals as necessary for democratisation) is itself perceived as a source of anxiety (loss, rootlessness) in a postmodern world. The well-meaning *Draft Convention for the Safeguarding of Intangible Cultural Heritage* also serves as a remedy for the global prioritising of tangible heritage and as a means to manage heritage. As this research shows, there is a great need for national heritage managers to critically reflect on the convention and to modify it for appropriate use in their country.

The concern with heritage is not simply for esoteric or psychological purposes. Heritage conservation is a potential source of income and is useful for the development of international ties. For Zanzibar, Seychelles and Mauritius contemporary forms of ICH identification and preservation entail the possibility of featuring on the World Heritage list (*World Culture Report* 2000) and of developing culture industries. However, adhering to or implementing the convention is not easy. At first glance, these difficulties are apparent in the practical, political and logistical issues faced by cultural heritage managers attempting to implement the convention. The latter are tasked with the communication, conservation, monitoring and development of ICH. It is a task that is made even more difficult by the fact that ICH is a term that is not easily communicated or translated. My past research in Mauritius (1999-2002) shows for example, that there is no word for it in Mauritian *Kreol* (the Creole dialect in Mauritius) or *Seychellois* (the Creole dialect of Seychelles) other than that which can be borrowed from French. Furthermore, UNESCO's endorsement of traditions that encourage benevolent interaction creates 'loopholes' for dominant groups who may decline to consider 'subordinate' cultural forms and draw on the 'fact' that they are disrespectful of gender rights or mutual respect.[15]

A closer look shows that in the case of Zanzibar, particular social dynamics complicate efforts to define heritage. Here, 'heritage' exists between groups, it is part of social process rather than being a 'gift' and it is informed by violence and globalisation. In my view, this will have specific implications in terms of the restitution, conservation, valuing and curating of what is considered as heritage. To this end, heritage protection regimes established to conserve the heritage of the colonised are problematic. Not only because they may suppress other ways of perceiving, knowing and being but also because they have the potential to subvert existing efforts to achieve peace. In the following, I offer brief discussions of the key issues focused on in the ethnographic chapters.

Anthropology, Violence and Globalisation

In a lecture on violence and peace, Nancy Scheper-Hughes (2001: 1) states that 'violence is not a natural topic for the anthropologist. Everything in our training and disposition trains us, like so many inverse bloodhounds, on the scent of the good in human life and society'. Heritage studies have tended to focus on 'the good in human life and society'. Heritage allows us to connect to our past and to celebrate what is good. It then becomes imperative to protect heritage, because we are preserving noble, creative human expressions. Wim van Binsbergen (2002) confirms this view when he argues that anthropologists of the 1930s and 1940s were focused on order and researched the conditions for non-violence, and were as Martin (1983) argues, blind to the violence of empire. From this perspective, violence was seen as social exception rather than the norm and relegated to deviants, to political or military crises or exotic peripheries that had not yet been 'pacified'. In the aftermath of World War Two, anthropologists like Gluckman (1955, 1963) and Coser (1956) began to write about the role of conflict in the constitution of society. Such studies suggested that violence was pervasive and sometimes integral to society. In the 1970s and 1980s the rising number of global and local conflicts encouraged some anthropologists (Campbell and Gibbs 1986, Feldman 1991, Riches 1986) to analyse violence as an increasingly normal aspect of social life in modern society. Also, around this time, anthropologists and sociologists begin to produce differentiated understandings of violence. One such study by Arthur Kleinman (1997) indicates varied forms of violence, distinguishing between social suffering, structural violence, social violence and political violence. Kleinman argues that these are often interrelated and interdependent, affecting the individual and their sense of self as part of a collective. Bauman's interesting (if somewhat dispassionate) work (1989) on the Holocaust reveals the close links between these different kinds of violence, which he says is the result of an ever-increasing obsession with rational efficiency, the central concern of modernity.

These 'cold' analyses of violence were criticised by a more reflective and reflexive group of anthropologists in the late 1980s and early 1990s. Writing about infanticide in the *favelas* of Brazil, Nancy Scheper-Hughes (1992) agreed with Bauman that there is an inextricable link between modernity and violence but argued (in her call for a more militant anthropology) that anthropologists do something about it. A few years later, van Binsbergen reflected on his research (violence and religious change in Zambia) and concluded that while anthropologists do need to critically reflect on their involvement in studies of violence, they also need to develop analytical frameworks that can assist either in the dissolution of conflict and violence or identify conditions under which peace can prevail. Writing about violence in general, he said that violence could now be perceived as 'an unexpected product of modernity'.

Reflections on the continuation of different kinds of violence in sub-Saharan Africa suggest that past experience of suffering can be interwoven with our present cultural expressions. In other words, violence is an integral product of history and contemporary experience. Secondly, people (especially those in subordinate positions who are usually the object of violence), develop behavioural and social strategies to cope with violence. To understand the nature of violence and responses to violence in a place like Zanzibar, one could look at Bourdieu's (1977, 1996) takes on the significance of everyday existence. He suggests that one looks beyond structural (formal, public) violence and observe 'mundane' symbolic expressions and events. One might also investigate the multiple outcomes of these interactions and symbolic expressions. My research suggests that in Zanzibar the 'outcomes' are evident in 'cool' politics. The latter is influenced not just by modernisation or globalisation but also by the historically embedded experience of violence.

Music

But there is more to these islands than the historical experience of oppression and violence. They have also forged culturally rich environments in which they have produced alternative hermeneutics and meta-languages that assist in multi-directional communication. As mentioned previously, heritage studies tend to focus on culturally bounded and presumed homogeneous cultural attributes. In Zanzibar, hybrid cultural expressions form an important part of social expression. This cultural crossroad produces a heritage conundrum for heritage scholars and managers. How does one preserve hybrid heritages? This is something that I found in looking at popular music forms in Zanzibar (*Taarab*). To understand the cultural complexity inherent in these modes of communication, I explored some of the theory of ethnomusicology.

The anthropological and linguistic paradigms that dominated ethnomusicology from the late nineteenth century to the 1960s have since been radically transformed. Approaches to the interpretation of music and its significance to society included the evolutionistic 'comparative musicology' developed by European scholars in the late nineteenth century, neo-functionalist studies (Alan Merriam 1964), behaviourist approaches (Alan Lomax 1968), structuralism (Pandora Hopkins 1977), and interpretivism (Timothy Rice 1986). Marxist influences on music theory and analysis in the 1970s and 1980s brought broader political considerations to ethnomusicology in the work of Feld (1983) and Seeger (1989) and in the critical political reflections on anthropological method and motivations (see Asad [1979], Fabian [1983] and Clifford [1986]). At around this time, semiotics also gained ground in reflections on form and politics in music (Boilès 1982, Nattiez 1975). This encouraged the study of other dimensions of popular music, especially that of performance. Specifically, ethnomusicologists and anthropologists (Coplan 1987) explored the socio-political implications of context and performance.

By the late 1980s and early 1990s postmodern ideas had influenced anthropologists' thoughts on the theory and articulation of music. Could music be an ongoing deliberative form of political action *and* a communicative arena for research subjects? In Chapter on Zanzibar, I discuss *taarab*, showing how 'external' politics and epistemologies continue to influence perspectives on and experiences of these music traditions and how subjective experiences and frameworks are disappearing. I argue that prejudicial views of the marginal groups that produce these music forms, new Afrocentric politics and economic necessity is encouraging such groups to abandon earlier music styles. I follow this with the argument that there is a deeper politics that is not always evident to cultural outsiders.

From this perspective (and as argued in empirical phenomenology) the 'research participant's 'reality' is not directly accessible to the researcher ... [and] the researcher's focus is thus neither on the phenomenon nor the participants, but rather on the dialogue of individuals with their contexts' (van der Mescht 2004: 2). Insight into this subjectively created world indicates the existence of a different politics of resistance and ideas about identity and heritage. These politics allow those performing and enjoying *Taarab* to produce particular forms of meaning.

Occupation Diversity

In the chapter on socialism and change in the Seychelles, I argue that occupation diversity is a major aspect of Seychellois existence but that political transformation in the 1970s meant that much of this was suppressed or not encouraged. In that chapter I offer some theoretical discussion of occupation diversity and show how (in the Seychelles at least), it is connected to cultural heritage.

5. Image and Commerce: Mauritius[16]

'Ou capave mange patrimoine ou?'[17]
In a paper on the role of the heritage industry in post-apartheid construction Ian Fairweather (2000) says that 'without culture there is no future'. In the new millennium one observes varying forms of culture and identity, where some groups emphasise the bounded nature of identity while others celebrate hybridisation. In postcolonial societies such as Mauritius, where the dominant majority perceive bounded identities as necessary for survival and prosperity, there are increasingly concerted efforts to reflect on group history as a means to promoting an authentic and homogeneous account of the past. The following discussion shows that the achievement of these objectives has not been easy because Creole identity is multifaceted and hybrid. However, in recent times, particular segments of Mauritian society have begun to impose their version of blackness on Creole identity so that an ideologically uncomplicated version of Creole culture and identity might be crafted.

The Focus on Heritage

In field research I found that the recent global and local focus on heritage is providing alternative and politically legitimate means to conquer space for identity purposes. UNESCO's National Commission in Mauritius is concerned to facilitate heritage initiatives. Mauritius also has a National Heritage Foundation (NHF) that has implemented a series of heritage preservation projects in the last three years. It is financially provided for via the National Heritage Trust Fund.

Heritage projects have been coming thick and fast since the setting up of the National Heritage Trust Fund in the Ministry of Arts and Culture. Writing about heritage management in general, Garrod and Fyall suggest that 'there is a strong emphasis on conservation [in heritage initiatives] ... fundamental task of the heritage sector must be to ensure an appropriate balance between the contemporary use of those assets and their conservation for the future' (Garrod and Fyall

2000: 682). Thus, there is a strong link between heritage tourism and the concept of sustainable development. In the following discussion I ask (with reference to Creoles) what kind of heritage is being preserved and what will it mean for the future of Creole identity.

In February 2004 there were international and virtual conferences in Mauritius on resistance, abolition and the importance of memory in slavery. That month the National Commission for UNESCO hosted the organisation's Director General, Koïchiro Matsuura. Together with the minister of Arts and Culture, Motee Ramdass, the Director General emphasised the importance of safeguarding cultural heritage and made a plea to Mauritius to ratify the Convention on Intangible Heritage. In an interview prior to the visit of the Director General the minister drew attention to Article 1, Clause 17 of the voted (October 2003) National Heritage Fund Bill, which states that 'Any person who unlawfully alters, damages, destroys, digs up, moves, changes, covers, conceals or any other way disfigures a national heritage shall commit an offence'.

My argument is: given that Creoles have not been in a position to publicly and tangibly articulate their history and identity and that for many centuries, the descendants of slaves have crafted their identity through oral tradition, dance and song, how are Creoles to participate in the process of heritage identification if the only means being offered is through the safeguarding of tangible heritage? For example, a maritime monument close to Mahebourg (a town historically associated with slaves on the east coast of Mauritius) commemorates the Dutch presence in and contributions to Mauritius. In the town itself are a few signposts indicating a slave presence on the island but these do not indicate their contributions to the society. Again, at Pointe Canon (also in Mahebourg) there is a monument (erected in 1985 and recently renovated) that commemorates the arrival of slaves in Mauritius. Here, there is a testimony to freedom but no information in the adjacent building about the cultural practices or social life of slaves. A similar lack of detail on slaves and their descendants is apparent at the recently inaugurated Blue Penny Museum at the Port Louis Waterfront. The museum celebrates the philately of Mauritius and provides an overview of the making of Port Louis. Nowhere in the exhibition is there mention of the slaves (or other labourers) that built the port and of the diverse ways in which they contributed to Port Louis society. Instead there is mention of Anglo- and Franco-Mauritian contributions including an elaborate exhibition on the story of Paul and Virginie, the Romeo and Juliet of white Mauritius. These 'silences' on black Mauritian identity and history are not going unnoticed. In a context where (tangible and intangible) heritage is creating a new playing field for representation, there are increasingly competing attempts to package blackness.

Rosabelle Boswell

The Role of Creole Organisations

At the time of my most recent research it was evident that local Creole activists and historians in Mauritius, some of whom have been deeply concerned with the silence on slave history and Creole society, have attempted to 're-package' Creole identity as a black and homogeneous identity. The re-packaging process is not new, it has been taking place over the past 30 years, especially in but not limited to the work pro-black movements and organisations such as Muvman Morisyen Kreol Afrikain (MMKA) the Movement for Black Mauritian Creoles; Mouvement Pour Le Progrés (Movement for Progress); Rassemblement Organisations Creoles (ROC) Union of Creole Organisations; and Organisation Fraternel (OF), a sort of Brothers in Arms. The latter, one of the oldest in Mauritius, emerged in the wake of nationwide ethnic riots in 1967 and initially had a religious base, similar to other ethnic movements on the island. Started by Sylvio Michel (then a young man destined for a Catholic seminary in France) and his brother Elie Michel, the organisation aimed to promote black consciousness in Mauritius and to draw attention to the plight of slave descendants on the island. OF (now known as the *Verts Fraternel* which emphasises not just political but also ecological awareness) has historically received the support of Creole clergy in Mauritius, especially those who preach a liberation gospel and are concerned to improve the situation of the mostly poor black Creoles living in impoverished villages and informal settlements. Together with organisations such as the OF, some Creole clergy have made public their aim to bring social justice to communities like Chamarel and Le Morne.

I argue that the public emancipation and consciousness raising process has intensified in the 1990s and is impacting differently on attempts to produce a homogeneous black identity. In 1993 a Creole Catholic priest (see Miles 1999) publicly reasserted the existence of a social malaise among Creoles in 1993. A few years later in 1998, several televised discussions at local conferences focused on the marginal situation of the descendants of slaves, and after the 1999 nationwide rioting (a Creole singer died under mysterious circumstances in police custody), public and media discussions of Creoles as a homogeneous group became more common. In my opinion, there are also increasingly assertive movements to reposition Creoles as the sole descendants of black-African slaves. These assertions are based on current reconstructions of slave and maroon history (Nagapen 1998 and Teelock 2001), where blackness and slave history are re-evaluated and Creoles are allocated an identity that implies greater homogeneity, particularly in terms of their experience of slavery.

These organisations and individuals are often in the public eye and have been focused on the identification or consolidation of tangible heritage. However other collectivities, highlighting intangible heritage and founded on a way of life (such as Rastafarianism), livelihood (hunting, fishing, cooking, brewing) or music, are not necessarily so. For me, these private or non-public collectivities which maintain the diversity and hybridity of Creole identity are presently not powerful enough to call for the public inscription of intangible culture. This was evident during fieldwork in two west coast villages, Chamarel and Le Morne.

The Valley of the Blacks?

Moustas, a Rasta living in Chamarel village on the southwest coast of Mauritius, is one of the few Rastafarians in Chamarel. Close friends with a non-Rasta, he lives with his wife and child in a secluded and simple concrete home in the village. He didn't tell me what made him become a Rastafarian except that when he chose that way of life, he 'finally saw the light' and 'was freed from wanting the things that others want but never get'. Moustas once asked me, 'What is the true name of my village?' When I answered he smiled a smile that seemed to suggest that I had been fooled like the 'rest of them'. 'No', he said shaking his massive dreads, 'the village and land beyond it is the Valley of the Blacks — this is where we came to liberate ourselves and we have to take the land back'. Moustas' response did not surprise me. I had heard similar statements from others who have been concerned to expunge the influence of 'white' civilisation from their personal and immediate environment. In Chamarel I also came across many storytellers, people who had once been hunters like ton Yves and young men who were honing their music skills. I also spoke to Marie-ange who told me about the recipes that her mother had passed on to her. This made me think about what Moustas meant by speaking about the 'Valley of the Blacks'. Was he referring specifically to slave or maroon history or was he alluding to a more diversified black African identity for Chamarel?

Thérèse Lamoureux, a Creole woman who has lived in Chamarel for most of her life, was a child when a group of African infantrymen hid in Chamarel during World War Two. She told me: 'They were so handsome and so smart many of our girls were smitten with them', and that her own brothers were recruited as infantrymen and sent to reinforce the Allied Forces in Egypt. Her words suggest that at that time Creole women and children did not necessarily see black people as victims but also believed them to be people of courage, value and discipline. In 2002, Thérèse was in her seventies. She also spoke about her eleven children, the many nights watching over them, and other peoples' children at parties held in the tiniest *cabane* (hut). Laughing, she said 'lizié pé blanc ar veille zénfants!'[18] I learned that the Creoles of Chamarel have a profound and diverse identity forged through interethnic contact, hunting, music making, cultivation and culinary skills. Speaking about this heritage, Thérèse said: 'barter was important for survival in Chamarel'. The 'hills' were known for their *Braconniers* who hunted and stole deer and pigs. Some would grow bananas and exchange these for fish with the fishermen from Le Morne and La Gaulette village. To go to church or parties known as Sega, *tambour* (drum Sega) people would walk down the escarpment in groups because it was completely dark at night. These parties were often performed in Case Noyale at the bottom of the escarpment. Young people walked up and down these hills to hear the music and dance. At the bottom of the hill they would stop by an Indian shop to buy tea and clean their shoes. On the way back up, some would pass by the local Chinese-owned trading store to buy scarce goods. This view of Creole history and heritage does not mesh particularly well with the view of 'blackness' and remoteness that can be sold to tourists. Moreover, it is a form of heritage that does not lend itself to being easily promoted in a society that is emphasising ethnic purity rather than mixture in its packaging of identities for tourist consumption.

Chamarel: The Cradle of Nature

To outsiders, the village of Chamarel is mostly known for its ecological bounty. Its seven-coloured earth is a product of old lavas produced between 3.5 and 7 million years ago (*Philips Atlas* 1994). This asset has attracted foreigners far and wide, and is turning Chamarel into an eco-tourist destination. The village itself stands between 200 and 400 metres above sea level (ibid: 17) and lies adjacent to the Black River Gorges National Park. The park contains indigenous ebony trees and a great variety of fauna. It stretches over two districts, the Black River District to the west and the Savanne District in the south. The village of Chamarel appears isolated to the newcomer. Transport to and from the place is infrequent and the village's location in a forested area makes it appear 'lost' and remote. Furthermore, with exception to several *tabagies* (shops selling basic foodstuffs and alcohol) there are no retailers of hardware or clothing nor is there a shopping complex, the latter being common (and a sign of modernity) in almost every town and village on the island. Chamarel has a Roman Catholic Church (Ste-Anne) that was built in 1876 it also has a town hall where several social activities occur.

Outsiders also know 'Chamarel' as a village once 'owned' by a white man, Charles Chazal de Chamarel, who obtained land concessions in the forested region in 1786. They also tend to associate the area with white landowning families. The history and heritage of these families is carefully preserved in an historical account of the region written by the historian Amedée Nagapen (1997). Today, the Creole inhabitants of the village cite these families as employers and landowners of uncultivated land where deer are raised and culled. These lands also form part of the thickly forested hills that lie adjacent to the Black River Gorges National Park. Verbal accounts of Chamarel that include the Creoles mention that the forests are closely guarded as Creole *Braconniers* (illegal hunters) often hunt the deer and Creoles plant their ganja there. In other words, from the outsider's point of view, Creole identity is marginal and Creoles are dangerous, reinforcing the colonial view of blackness as the source of evil. In Nagapen's account of Chamarel, there is little mention of the Creoles living in the village, except for when they redeemed themselves by performing a brave deed or showed their worth by converting to Christianity.

I found a lack of authoritative accounts on the history and social life of Creoles living in Chamarel and the present and continued economic marginalisation of Creoles in Mauritian society has encouraged outsiders to package blackness in the village mostly for tourist consumption. This is being achieved through the reification of Chamarel village as a backward village where nature has taken over. Such a view has, in my opinion, dire consequences for Creoles and their identity in this village. On the surface, it seems that the casting of Chamarel as a place of nature is elevating it as a village where people have discovered the secret of good living in a rapidly modernising state. On the other hand (and more realistically) it confirms residents as being atavistic. In the 1950s for example, young women living in the village of Chamarel were highly sought after as domestic workers by urbanites, in particular, Chinese business people in Port Louis. It was believed that these women make good domestic workers because they are servile, meek and unfamiliar with the urban environment. In many instances, workers from Chamarel were described as atavistic through references made about them being *zako Chamarel* — Chamarel monkeys. I would argue that the pervasive portrayal of the village as undeveloped and the continued association of its residents with nature forms part of a less visible agenda that promotes a negative view of blackness, one based on the lack of progress and on primitiveness. This was apparent during fieldwork, when residents spoke about Chamarel being symbolically a part of the furthest, darkest 'interior'. The construction of Chamarel as a cradle of nature and its people as rural and primitive encouraged me to see 'nature is simultaneously real, collective, and discursive — and needs to be naturalized, sociologized and deconstructed accordingly' (Escobar 1999: 2). Furthermore, the reification of Chamarel village as a cradle of nature is *visibly* congruent with the tourist investors' efforts to identify leisure spaces further inland, the ministry of tourism's objective to reduce pressure on coastal resources and the Mauritius Wildlife Fund's efforts to preserve fauna and flora in the National Park. The recent conversion of some private land adjacent to the park into an adventure park also reaffirms the view of Chamarel as a place of nature.

In the new millennium, nature has also become a vital financial resource. Promoting Chamarel as a place of nature could provide work for the local population but in 2004, this was not apparent. Speaking to residents in the village I was told that few people are employed in the adventure park and that many were still waiting for government to implement its eco-tourism plans. The Mauritian government's environmental conservation and management efforts in Chamarel appear to be influenced by tourist demand for ecologically responsible tourism. So much so that in the case of Chamarel they are prepared to cast inhabitants as rural and traditional in order for the people to fit in with the developers' view of it as 'a remote village lost in nature'.

In 2001, the Ministry of Tourism proposed the 'Chamarel Integrated Development Project' (CIDP). While this project aimed to meet tourist and ecological conservation demands it risks packaging a particular identity for Creoles in the village, one premised on a largely negative view of blackness. The main objectives of the project were cited as follows:

- To enhance tourism enjoyment and boost up tourist spending with spill-over effects for the village;

- To diversify the tourism product by developing rural and cultural tourism; to involve local people for sustainable development of the tourism industry;

- To create employment and enable local people to reap the benefits of tourism; and

- To upgrade the physical environment of a deprived village and improve the standard of living of the inhabitants.

The Ministry described the village as follows:

Chamarel is a small deprived village, situated in the South West of the island, isolated in the middle of dense forest and mountains with sugar cane fields over a large area. It has a population of about six hundred inhabitants and one hundred and sixty-three households (Ministry of Economic Development, Productivity and Regional Development Central Statistical Office) ...

Chamarel offers to visitors a splendid panoramic view of the green landscape with Mount Le Morne, which stands on the horizon merging with the blue sea. Chamarel encompasses all the characteristics of a remote village lost in nature which offers an ideal place for rural, cultural, and eco-tourism.

In keeping with the view of Chamarel as a remote, rural and ecologically significant village, the project creators emphasised rural or rustic activities for the inhabitants. They suggested that a craft village be created 'where visitors could witness the manufacture of handicrafts along with effecting direct purchases from artisans [and that these] products would include basketry, textiles, wooden sculptures and other types depending on the availability of appropriate raw materials in the village'. In 2000 and 2001, several women in Chamarel learned various craftwork techniques so that they could be employed in the forthcoming craft village. The project would emphasise the rustic and natural aspect of life in Chamarel along with the 'naturalness' of craftwork among the women. My fieldwork suggests that except for the mention of wooden sculptures, the range of traditional products made in the village does not include the items suggested by the Ministry. Chamarel residents are, however, skilled at brewing alcoholic drinks, sourcing traditional medicines, preparing food made from ingredients drawn from vegetation found in Chamarel, hunting, entertaining and producing music.

In 2001, it seemed that the culinary skills of the inhabitants might become useful if the third suggestion in the CIDP proposal is implemented. The proposal of *Table d'Hotes*[19] should, according to the proposers, 'enable visitors to discover the inner life of the island, meet the inhabitants in their natural habitat and discover Mauritian recipes. The *Table d'Hotes* would contribute to the development of cultural tourism and would enable the local people to reap the economic benefits of tourism'. But in 2004, I found that out of the twelve tenders submitted to government for these local restaurants, only two were approved. Both of these restaurants belong to people who are already financially established in the village and, as one of my interviewees argued, 'they are not even providing local fare'.

How have discussions on the ecological conservation been received by the inhabitants of Chamarel? Most of the older residents interviewed were positive about the village becoming a site for eco-tourism. Most of them were nostalgic about the past and expressed a wish to keep Chamarel 'as natural as possible' because 'we are used to life like this'. However, younger residents expressed their concern that Chamarel residents were being forced 'back in time' when in actual fact there are other skills that could be emphasised to bring tourists to the area. For example, some mentioned that in Chamarel there are sculptors, musicians and entertainers but that these skills and requests to cater for these skills are not being considered. Instead, specific elements of a 'natural' existence and tangible heritage are being emphasised in Chamarel and effort is being made to revitalise an image of the place as a remote haven for eco-tourists. This is having the effect of re-traditionalising the residents and packaging blackness in a way that does not leave room for modernity and inter-ethnicity.

The Descendants of Maroons?

If Chamarel is perceived as the nature lover's paradise, Le Morne village is the freedom fighter's 'dream'. Tucked away behind the monolith of Le Morne it is a small village historically associated with liberation. Its inhabitants are perceived as independent souls that depend on fishing to survive. It is in Le Morne village that I met fisherwomen for the first time, and where four of them challenged outsiders' view of the village. Here, women and children wade out into the water as the tide is going out, to collect *ti moules*[20] for supper late on summer evenings. Laughing, one of the fisherwomen indicated the independent lives of some women in the village by telling me that while men do not like that they fish, the sea is more dependable than men could ever be. According to *ton* Michel, another Creole resident, Le Morne village only became a distinctive settlement in 1979 after the first government of Mauritius built houses for those who were living there. But before this time, many had been living in the maroon village of *Trou Chenille*, whose traces are still to be found on a slope of Le Morne. There, the descendants of maroon slaves and those newly manumitted built a community where music, dancing and oratory played a vital role in the sustenance of solidarity. When *ton* Michel and his family arrived in Le Morne village many of these musical and oral traditions continued, and shaped local identity juxtaposing it with the identity of Creoles living elsewhere on the island. This was very evident at the time of my research. Current impositions of particular identities on these villages (as eco-tourism or fishing villages) highlight contemporary struggles over representation and Creole identity in Mauritius. Initially *ton* Michel[21] reinforced the view of Le Morne as a site of freedom:

On *montagne*[22] Morne there lived many escaped slaves, but there is no memory for them. It is as though nothing happened there. But I know that something did. There is a small valley on the mountain slope, where there was once a village. My grandfather told me how the first inhabitants got there. There were many shipwrecks in those days and one of them foundered on the east coast at Les pointes des Hollandais, close to Grand Port in Mahebourg. The slaves that had survived the journey were strong, stronger than their captors and while the white men drowned, some of the blacks managed to swim ashore. When they got there, some of them were recaptured, some of them believed that the white men would eat them and ran away. Only a few survived, but with great courage they travelled along the southern wild coastline and settled in the mountain.

Spending more time with *ton* Michel I learned about the hardships experienced by Creoles in their resettlement in Le Morne village and also their interdependence with non-Creoles, stories that varied narratives about the Creoles' past. Food shortages during World War Two, for instance, meant that locals had to depend on maize as their staple food. *Ton* Michel tells me that the Indians cultivated the maize and that a local Chinese shopkeeper owned a maize mill. It was *ton* Michel's task to crush the maize in this machine. He often readjusted it so that it would spit out extra grains for the children of the destitute to collect for food. His stories as well as those of *Ti*[23] Roland contribute to identity formation among Creoles, but they are not, as Nuttall and Coetzee (2000: 14) argue, based on specific accounts of the past that privilege 'a few master narratives that offer a sense of unity at the cost of ignoring the fracture and dissonance'. *Ti* Roland, born in 1931 in the village of Trou-Chenille, says that he had a wonderful childhood there and after his family was forced to move to Le Morne, his octopus fishing skills helped to develop the family's exchanges with Chinese families living in the village. His stories further confirm the fact of substantive interethnic contact and exchange in the village.

Heritage Projects in the Le Morne Region

If Chamarel is being re-ruralised and re-traditionalised, the reverse is happening to Le Morne village. In the last twenty years, five hotels have been constructed on the Le Morne peninsula, and one of these, *Le Paradis*, occupies a seven kilometres stretch of land. By 2004, the government had approved plans submitted by the private enterprise of Rogers Group to commence a resort scheme development on the southern slope of Le Morne. There are currently further plans for integrated tourism schemes along the southwest coastline, such as the development in the south of part of Bel Ombre sugar estate land into a golf estate and the location of several hotels. Rapid hotel development is concealing, altering and in some instances destroying intangible heritage. One of these even pretends to support heritage efforts and is being named the *Heritage Golf and Spa Resort*.

Long-term residents in the area that I spoke to perceive the sea, their stories and music as a fundamental part of their history and heritage and are concerned that efforts were not being made to conserve these resources. The above-mentioned developments have heralded the arrival of water sports, golfing and deep-sea fishing that are rapidly killing off marine life in the peninsula and are threatening the safety net that fishing provides for many of the families living there. Furthermore (and according to my interviews) tourism development in the area has employed a minority of the young people living in the area. This suggests that there are no viable economic, symbolic and social alternatives being offered to the people living in Le Morne.

History, as told from the perspective of Creoles living in Le Morne, and local cultural practice, are important for the liberation of suppressed or silenced cultural discourses. By interrogating the existing narrative of events, some Creole activists and revisionist historians are seeking to lift the silence on the Creoles' slave past, but at the same time they are articulating a more homogeneous identity for Creoles.

In 2004, on the southwest coast of Mauritius, blackness was not being packaged but obliterated. Recreational and eco-tourism development is concealing the presence of black Creoles in the forging of these communities. And, although protesters from the OF, MMKA, NHF and MWF, opposed the development of cable car facilities on Le Morne in 1999, the private sector seems to be winning. It was not the first time that the people of Le Morne village have protested against tourism development in the environs of their village. In 1998, they successfully prevented Les Pavillons hotel from appropriating a major part of their public beach (*Week-end*, 21 November 2000). And, where tourism development occurs at an unprecedented rate and largely at the expense of nationals, the local population has been known to vociferously oppose further development or to severely criticise the state. This is certainly the case in the Caribbean, where Polly Pattullo's (1996) research revealed that the black populations on those islands were feeling like 'aliens' in their own land. This was apparent in 2000 when there were plans to develop tourist facilities on mount Le Morne.

The proposed development, spearheaded by Innovative Leisure Limited, involved the development of a cable car and helipad on mount Le Morne. In December 2000, the developer Francis Piat had been sued by the MWF for the destruction of rare flora on the mountain but not sued for going ahead in obliterating a major part of Creole heritage. Responding to this, Piat said, 'I am being sued for 38 trees. This is happening while I am setting up a nursery that will produces 3,800, then 38,000, and ultimately 38 million young trees of the rarest species. This will help to save not only the ecosystem on top of Le Morne, but everywhere else where they have disappeared or are disappearing across the country' (*News on Sunday*, 30 April 2000). The tourism potential of this project encouraged the government to reflect favourably on the project:

With the court's favourable verdict, the promoters now expect things to move as they consider that this project is in line with government's policy of promoting eco-tourism as well as with UNESCO's plan to encourage duty towards history. The project is expected to generate some 100 jobs during its initial stage of operation (*News on Sunday*, 29 June 2001: 1).

The *News on Sunday* journalists reported on their interview (ibid) with Piat and the latter's discussions of his broader objectives for the Le Morne project. Here Piat argued that he had 'become a staunch advocate of a re-writing of Mauritian history in favour of the Creole community' (ibid). This comment suggests that private investors are well aware of the symbolic importance of Le Morne and use it as a means to detract public attention from their real intentions. There are plans for the construction of a resort on the southern slope of Le Morne mountain. This suggests that tourist development is going ahead on a part of the mountain and that investors like Francis Piat have not seriously considered local opposition to any development on the mountain. It is possible that the government of Mauritius will (as a way of obtaining both material and symbolic currency) attempt to nominate Le Morne as a 'mixed' (tourist and cultural site) for UNESCO's World Heritage List.

For four years, plans for Le Morne have unleashed a series of heated debates about the position of Creole history and identity in Mauritius (see K. Agorsah, *Week-end*, 21 November 2000), V. Teelock (*l'Express*, 24 April 2000) and S. Selvon (*News on Sunday*, 30 April 2000: 14). But there has been little reflection on the deeper ramifications of a particular form of heritage tourism in the country — one that emphasises boundaries rather than interaction and commonalities. After the visit of Matsuura, Mauritians debated whether Le Morne or Aapravasi Ghat would be included on UNESCO's World Heritage List. To my knowledge, there has been little or no mention of the preservation of intangible heritage in Mauritius. Thus heritage projects concerning the experiences, livelihood and the historical settlement of slaves have not been considered yet. The focus is still on tangible heritage and even that is being portrayed as homogeneous.

In an interview (*l'Express* 24 April 2000: 10) on Le Morne, the historian Vijaya Teelock says that '*Le Morne symbolise la lutte pour l'independence, la lutte contre la colonisation, la lutte pour la liberté*', (the Morne symbolises the fight for independence, the fight against colonisation, the fight for liberty). This view of Le Morne as a symbol of freedom is important to the nation-building process by its encouragement of genuine cultural dialogue through a reviewing of the island's slave past. However, it also serves to undermine nation building and democracy by suppressing a range of narratives about Creole and Mauritian identity. In the new millennium, the concern to locate Creole identity in Mauritian society indicates that there are various forms of identity reconstruction taking place among Creoles. Some believe that assimilation is the only way and are making a concerted effort to become 'respectable'. In Chamarel this is involving the acceptance of eco-tourism initiatives and the recasting of residents as rural and traditional. In other words, becoming respectable involves accepting one's positioning in the market economy. Others like Moustas, *ton* Yves, *ton* Michel, *ti* Roland and Thérèse are exploring diverse and sometimes hybridised identities on the path to self-definition. This is allowing them a means of liberation and a means to express their diverse and hybrid heritage. However, proponents of a slave and Afrocentric discourses in Mauritius are suppressing these identities and risk entrenching primordialism among Creoles.

My argument in this chapter is that there is much more to the heritage and identity of the residents of Le Morne village than Mount Le Morne, just as there is more to the heritage and identity of those living in Chamarel than nature. In Le Morne for example, residents attach great importance to Mount Le Morne and the fact that it is a symbol of Creole liberation and power. Conscious of increasing difficulty in the portrayal of their diverse experiences, one of my Creole interviewees in the east coast village of Flacq summed up the *status quo* by saying '*Nu aussi nu bizin zwé nu filme*'.[24] What she meant by this is that more Creoles have to participate in projects to revise Mauritian history and to locate the historical settlements and sites that are significant to the history of slavery and indenture so that Creoles might occupy more space in the local cultural hierarchy. In other words, they must participate in the homogenising of their identity if they are to obtain resources and a stronger position in Mauritian society. Not all Creoles, however, are convinced this strategy will bring tangible rewards. As one Le Morne resident said, 'Ou capave mange patrimoine ou?' (Can you eat 'heritage?).

Conclusion

In a protest against the cable car plans for Le Morne mountain, Kofi Agorsah, an archaeologist, expressed the view (*l'Express* 21 November 2000) that 'The portrait of freedom fighters that emerges in Black history is often complex and contradictory and illustrate that human history has always involved the creation of a recognised status in societies as a means of denying rights and privileges to particular societies. The records about their struggles are often ignored, distorted or misrepresented so that they could be exploited for social, political and economic purposes'. Agorsah's words suggest that the descendants of slaves have a diverse history and experience that needs to be articulated. In 2004 both villages were experiencing change brought on by the growing tourism industry in Mauritius. In 2004 resort development on the southern slope of Le Morne was going ahead and a private eco-tourism adventure park had been opened close to Chamarel. The expansion of tourism, while perceived as necessary by both the public and private sector, risks destroying the very assets that foreign tourists desire and major cultural organisations such as UNESCO seek. In Mauritius, heritage projects are becoming a part of the ongoing conquest of space on a very small island. As Papastergiadis (1997) notes in his analysis of hybridity and identity, in states like Mauritius, uncertain origins, multiple historical narratives and mixed blood give rise to notions of contamination, impurity and weakness. The preservation of cultural heritage is primarily seen as means to maintain bounded identity.

Recent interrogations of identity are also meaning that heritage tourism is becoming a way of dealing with the memory and experience of the past. For the Creoles, this is currently involving an encounter with the memory and experience of slavery. In my view, this encounter with the past should also involve an acknowledgement of the diversity of experience and the hybridity of Creoles. Once a particular version of the truth about the past is impressed on a landmark like Le Morne the generations to come may see that impression as the truth about the place or believe that Le Morne is the only significant element of their heritage. Similarly, embedding the residents of Chamarel in a bio-centric landscape limits the cultural expressions of the residents and suppresses their diverse skills and identities.

In the long term, attempts at homogenisation may have real, material effects in that they might destroy sustainable livelihoods. In both Chamarel and Le Morne village, powerful financial and political interests are already influencing the capacity of the locals to articulate local history and identities. The homogenisation of Creole history and experience, while important for the cultural ideal of a bounded group with a definite history, suppresses a range of local narratives about Creole identity and reality, necessary for authentic intercultural dialogue.

In the following chapter I consider issues of heritage management in Zanzibar. The information presented is based on research conducted between 2003 and 2005. Further work is envisaged (from 2007) where a more detailed account of local perspectives on and experiences of heritage will be recorded.

6. Violence and Compromise: Zanzibar

Le passé n'est pas mort, ce n'est même pas passé[25]

Introduction

In 2000, UNESCO nominated Stone Town (Unguja's main port city) a World Heritage site. Three years later, at the UNESCO General Conference in Paris (in October 2003), the 120 members voted unanimously for a new international convention aimed at the protection of intangible cultural heritage (ICH), defined as music, tales, rituals, systems of folk knowledge and epics. To date, existing cultural organisations in Zanzibar have not taken the initiative to identify local ICH for the Representative List of the Intangible Cultural Heritage of Humanity.

In this chapter, I document some of my research findings in Zanzibar, focusing on violence and globalisation as two challenges to ICH identification and management[26] on the islands. I argue that these have contradictory effects on ICH in Zanzibar and need to be critically reflected upon by those interested in heritage preservation and promotion. In one sense, both are disruptive and have the potential to suppress particular cultural forms. However, responses to these may also encourage and sustain cultural forms and modes of cultural transfer. One response, 'cool politics' (basically an openness to exchange, bricolage and hybridisation), often seen as a barrier to ICH identification, has made space for violence in the creation of creolised and 'mixed' cultural forms. I argue that any consideration of ICH preservation in Zanzibar needs to include reflection on the role of this complex and violent history in social interaction and cultural expression. Are UNESCO's current approaches to tangible and intangible heritage feasible in this complex and precarious social world?

Let me begin by arguing that being 'subaltern' produces particular experiences of violence (in its different forms) and encourages specific strategies to respond to violence. For example, my own life experiences (in Mauritius and Malawi) helped me to notice (even if at least on a very superficial level) the salience of everyday violence and some of the very different ways in which people were dealing with it in Zanzibar. Initial conversations with residents suggested that structural and political violence is an important source of suffering that can impede meaningful engagement in social life. Closer observation is revealing that social suffering (as a sort of extended post-traumatic stress disorder) continues to affect social interaction and expression in a more fundamental way. Viewed from afar, it is not only ritual or musical expressions that are contributing to the perpetuation of this state of affairs. Memory projects implemented by heritage regimes provide the tangible form through which such violence can be remembered and re-inflicted. As an outsider, I experienced a sort of indirect terror by visiting the dark cells underneath the Anglican Church (built on top of the old slave market in the heart of Stone Town) or whenever I walked past the police building, Mambo Msiige, in Stone Town. The foundations of the latter are said to be filled with the bodies of slaves who were buried alive there, as it was believed that human blood strengthened foundations. Thus in encouraging the sustenance of slave architecture and history, slave descendants are regularly made painfully and violently aware of their history of victimisation, are expected to accept it as 'their' history and to encounter it 'cold'. As Dirk Hoerder points out in his discussion of subalterneity, the subaltern is expected to 'observe closely, to learn and to fit in' (2003: 26). Thus 'cool' politics is not about compromise, it is a way to accommodate violence and oppression and to resist it without incurring further direct violence.

In the following, I argue that heritage managers need to be thoroughly aware of the complex interplay between violence and globalisation and the unique social dynamics that it might produce in 'exotic peripheries'. A first step would involve a critical review of the concept of heritage.

Heritage in Stone Town

The nomination of Stone Town as a World Heritage site occurred rather late in the history of heritage preservation. UNESCO's concern with heritage can be traced back to the 1972 ratification of the Convention for the Protection of the World Cultural and Natural Heritage, a normative and standard-setting instrument for the management of heritage. Since then, more than 721 sites have been inscribed on the World Heritage list. However, they are mostly 'tangible' heritage (monuments, archaeological sites, museums) and are to be found overwhelmingly in Europe and North America. As Bouchenaki reports in his discussion of heritage, 'It took until 1982 for UNESCO to set up a 'Committee of Experts on the Safeguarding of Folklore' and create a special 'Section for the Non-Physical Heritage', resulting in the Recommendation on the Protection of Traditional Culture and Folklore, adopted in 1989' (www.unesco.org). This set a precedent for the recognition of traditions and folklore. In 1998, a UNESCO committee adopted a regular reporting system on the WHC (World Heritage Convention). To date, thirty-seven African states have signed the WHC. The committee is tasked with updating information on heritage preservation, evaluating whether WHC values continue to be upheld, and developing mechanisms for regional cooperation and capacity building. In Africa and Asia there is a wealth of 'intangible' heritage that is unaccounted for. With the new international convention it seems that UNESCO aims to make heritage identification and preservation more democratic, participatory and a means to alleviate poverty. To achieve this goal, the organisation hopes to develop a programme in Africa in 2009 that will build local capacity in heritage management. It is envisaged that this will involve raising awareness about heritage, and providing training and the sharing of expertise and information on heritage management.

There are many issues to consider in the study of ICH management in Zanzibar. In the first instance, there is the division of the population along racial and ethnic lines. This is evident in the long-term animosity between mainlanders and islanders and Africans and Arabs that, in part, continue to fuel political resentment. Towards the end of the brief ethnographic discussion, I argue that it is only really those who have resources in urban Zanzibar that are able to reflect on the significance and varied potential of ICH management in their country. Second, poverty is a major factor in the lives of Zanzibaris, most of those I met during research were deeply concerned about survival. The following ethnographic data show that for many Zanzibaris and mainland Tanzanians there are more immediate concerns than the preservation and management of cultural heritage. Rural Zanzibaris, in particular, are substantively affected by poverty, ill health and basic educational deficiencies on the island. Third is the threat of violence. The national elections in 2005 brought with them the ever-present threat of violence from the CCM-backed police and military on the island. Zanzibaris currently fear for their lives and safety as confrontations between CCM and CUF supporters increase.

Fourthly, the fieldwork data showed that Zanzibar is a profoundly mixed society and that most heritages are perceived as mixed. And fifth, Zanzibar is part of a third world state; it is still heavily influenced by external (Western) political and cultural discourses. However, it has its own epistemologies that are forged by its unique history and population. Then there is the issue of commercialisation. Not all ICH can be promoted or preserved in a way that does not involve 'de-authentication'. The maintenance of authenticity is a major aspect of dominant views on ICH. At the Zanzibar International Film Festival (ZIFF) 2004, some Zanzibari and other east African musicians argued that for efficiency, autonomy and protection of their intellectual property they would rather establish partnerships with international investors than state-run organisations that might not always be concerned with culture preservation. Further research is needed to establish whether these international investments are not reducing 'the work's faithfulness to itself, its origins and environment'.[27] Another issue is whether 'worthy' forms of intangible heritage (once identified) can be 'managed' in such a way as to obviate discussions of its origins or foundations entirely. For example, violence and oppression has inspired different music forms in Zanzibar. How will UNESCO reflect the role of violence in social constitution without compromising its moral stance on cultural preservation?

Fieldwork in Zanzibar

Mainlanders versus Islanders

The first monsoon rains (*mvuli*) were coming to an end when I first travelled to Zanzibar. On the plane to Dar-es-Salaam (Dar), I met a Tanzanian woman who had come to South Africa for cancer treatment. She told me that she was a lecturer in business management and that she was teaching at a college in northern Tanzania and was now on her way home to see her family, after having spent three weeks undergoing radiotherapy in Johannesburg (her family lives in a small village not far from the Ngorongoro crater, the edge of the Maasai Mara). Bella (that was her name) asked where I was going and when I said Zanzibar, she told me that the Zanzibaris are friendly up to a point. 'They like to distinguish between themselves and ordinary Tanzanians, they keep themselves "apart" from us'. Bella then went on to tell me that Tanzanians (Zanzibaris included) benefited from the 1964 Revolution. Women like her benefited from socialist politics as educational institutions focused on employment equity and the advancement of women in Tanzanian society. She noted that the process of women's empowerment could have been managed better as many women were still largely illiterate and isolated after the revolution, and that recently poverty and AIDS had encouraged them to mismanage loans received from the state and international banking institutions.

Bella argued that Zanzibaris had not really made use of the resources offered by the state. After the 1964 Revolution (which led to the unification of Tanganyika and Zanzibar islands), each Tanzanian willing to take up cultivation received three acres of land and basic support from the government. She told me to look out for Zanzibari laziness: 'you'll notice it', she said, 'by looking at their uncultivated *shambas*'. Once at Dar international airport, the presence of armed men in military uniform walking around the relatively empty airport and pictures of both the Zanzibari and Tanzanian president made me overtly aware of deep divisions within the Tanzanian government and of government attempts to impose identity on Tanzanians and Zanzibaris. Having experienced a similar situation in Malawi in the 1980s, I felt unhappily familiar with the dilapidated state of the infrastructure and nervous about the men with guns. For a while we were 'locked' up in our respective departure lounges until it was time for us to board our next flight to Unguja. I watched as two guards used a border collie and another dog of indeterminate origin to patrol the premises.

The experience of uneasiness and sense of being controlled was also evident after arriving in Zanzibar. The main road leading to the east coast of the island, known locally as *Bububu*, (so named because of the sound of steam trains travelling down the previously existing track), is marked by numerous police barriers. Drivers going out to the tourist hotels (on the east coast) have to show their daily permits in order to proceed. Without these permits, they cannot carry on with their journey to the eastern part of the island. Many of the *daladala* (local taxi) drivers would appear more nervous as we approached a police barrier and one driver in particular told me, 'don't say a word when we pass the police. They won't know that you're not Zanzibari if you don't speak'. Afterwards, I asked him why he had wanted me to stay quiet. He answered that he had not renewed his day permit and the police often looked for 'any excuse' to harass 'them', meaning the Zanzibaris.

In David Parkin's (2001) account of Zanzibar during and after the 1995 and 2000 general elections, he focuses on political and structural violence as a source of division between mainlanders and islanders. Two parties, the majority Chama Cha Mapinduzi or CCM (The Revolutionary Party) founded in 1964, and the Civic United Front or CUF that emerged after the 1964 Revolution, dominate the political landscape. CUF supporters are mostly from Pemba. They are people of Omani descent and followers of Ibadi Islam, and CCM supporters are from mainland Tanzania, are of African descent and are Christian or Sunni/Shi'ite Muslims. Speaking to Bella about political parties in Tanzania, she confirmed the importance of rumours and gossip to politicking on the island. She said that she had 'heard a rumour that [the president of semi-autonomous Zanzibar] was the nephew of the founder of the CUF', suggesting not only that the president of Zanzibar might put family interests first but also that they (the Zanzibari Arabs) are prone to nepotism. The animosity and political competition between CUF and CCM supporters is evident in the numerous attacks on CUF supporters in 1995 and 2001, including the attack perpetrated on an east coast tourist establishment in 2001 because the owner, an outspoken CUF supporter, had dared to voice her objection to CCM tactics in public. Parkin notes that the CCM is seen as a mainland party that is seeking to 'Africanise' Zanzibaris through the destruction of Arab businesses and the torture and rape of the Arab minority. My interviews in Zanzibar also suggested that the CCM is doing this through the encouragement of (mainland style) Swahili on the island and through the Tanzanian state's assimilation of Afro-Shirazi/Omani cultural forms such as Taarab music. Closer observation indicates that there are other forms of violence in Zanzibar, the kind that is (perhaps) longer lasting and denies the humanity of those considered as the 'other'.

They're Lazy, We're Not

From Stone Town to Kiwengwa along Bububu road on the east coast of Unguja there are various villages: Mahonda (the site of a disused sugar factory that ran out of spare parts), Mfeniseni (jackfruit village) and Kinyasini, where there are small fields of rice. Closer to Stone Town, as the night began to fall, families came out of their houses and shops to sit outside in their courtyards. Even at night, residential areas and shopping areas on the edge of Stone Town were alive with shoppers and traders. When I asked Seif (one of my interviewees) when these shops close, I was told: 'only when the people decide to sleep'. This answer suggested that the Zanzibaris are keen to trade for as long as possible so as to make a decent living. The humidity of the island also encouraged people to stay outdoors as long as they could. Inside, a small concrete dwelling or a house made of mud and *makuti* (palm thatching) leaves, could be too warm to bear. The further we got from Stone Town, the darker it became. Small clusters of thatched clay and mud houses occasionally came into sight as the light from the van fell upon them. From time to time we passed men on bicycles, their only source of light being torches that they held while gripping the handlebars. The only places with electricity seemed to be the police stations.

The high level of formal unemployment (there are no industries on Zanzibar island), is a source of concern among residents and a cause for tension between islanders and mainlanders. Reflecting on this, Seif said that 'we see development in Dar and Arusha. There they have fine tall buildings and nothing in

Zanzibar. Stone Town is just an old town. Other than "keeping" this town, there is nothing else for us'. This is the reason, Seif continued, that there was a need for fresh negotiations with the majority political party CCM. He also added that 'anyway, the people are tired of waiting'. The lack of formal employment did not appear to deter Zanzibaris from devising their own livelihood. From early morning until late at night, all along the road from Kiwengwa to Stone Town, cultivators were busy either tending to family rice fields or banana plots. Near Mahonda (the site of the disused sugar factory), some men had set up manual cane crushers and spent their time crushing the cane brought in by others who cultivated cane as part of their livelihood. Some families also keep cattle and on any given day one can see the milk sellers riding into town with milk urns strapped to the back of their bicycle.

Closer to the coast, small settlements have set up coral crushing industries. The coral is used for building and whitewashing. The crushing of coral is labour intensive and the entire family is involved. Adult males hammer the larger pieces of coral into palm-sized stones and children are tasked with reducing smaller stones into fine coral powder. On the east coast, villagers mostly fish for a living. The fishermen make use of *ngalawas* (outrigger canoes reminiscent of the kind found in Pacific island communities and confirming the historical presence of Austronesians in this region) made usually of one hollowed out mango tree. These are light and swift in the water, enabling them to go out on the reef without disturbing the live coral below. In the early 1990s, women along the east coast, and particularly in Kiwengwa village, began to plant and harvest seaweed that is ultimately sold on the Chinese market. By the time that I arrived in Kiwengwa village (on the north east coast of the island), the women there said that they were not earning much from the sale of seaweed, which in any case was a labour intensive and precarious livelihood, easily ruined by strong tides and increasing numbers of *ngalawas* and tourist boats.

General observations of Zanzibaris at work suggested that they were not lazy at all, that they were often passionate about work and were creative in their attempts to earn a living. However, a common distinction made between mainlanders and islanders is that islanders (particularly those of African descent) are lazy, backward and not really capable of benefiting from the Tanzanian government's efforts to develop the island.

Explaining the mainland/island dichotomy and the nature of identity and culture in Zanzibar, Imruh Bakari, then (in 2004) the director of the Zanzibar International Film Festival (ZIFF), said to me: 'the islands have their own dynamic. They are islands'. By saying this, Imruh was suggesting that it is difficult for mainlanders to understand islanders. The latter have a tendency to seek and to express their autonomy because of the nature of the territory in which they live. At the same time, islanders acknowledge that they have things in common with one another, even if this involves a shared history of oppression and terror. Imruh went on to say that 'Islanders and mainlanders parody the differences between them. The more that you look at their differences from the perspective of performance and parody, the more you will understand identity in this place. Here, people like to talk about their "roots" and they make a big deal of it, just to show that they are different, but they all know that they are of mixed ancestry, some of it dating back to the eighth century!' Thus, according to Imruh it only *appears* that islanders and mainlanders are radically different from each other because of the extent to which difference is parodied and performed in public. Imruh seemed to be arguing that there are no significant differences between islanders and mainlanders and that even if there are long-existing tensions between those of Arab and African descent, Zanzibar is a hybridised social space.

Let me take his argument further. It is possible to say that the hybridised space of Zanzibar is not a *fait accompli* and needs to be continually constituted for a measure of peace to be maintained. In the course of its history, this process has been assisted by a series of events — for example, the settling of the islands by people from Oman, Persia, India and Africa. Recently, Zanzibaris have had to make a conscious effort to promote 'cool' politics, particularly in the face of homogenisation by the dominant political party. However, this politics cannot always be achieved through references to politically uncomplicated events or histories. Therefore in *Taarab*, the popular music of Zanzibar, we find lamentations and oblique references to violence and oppression. We also find the use of diverse instruments indicating the mixed nature of the society. All of these indicate that Taarab serves as a point of conversion for the different (but similarly affected) groups on the island.

The Politics of Taarab

Zanzibar has many different kinds of music and traditions. Islanders often make a distinction between *Taarab* (orchestra & poetry-style music) and *Ngoma* (drumming), emphasising regional, racial and political differences. However, variations exist within each and they indicate the complex form of music and the diversity of audiences that enjoy it.[28] Taarab is often discussed as the national music of Zanzibar. It draws its influences from the Arab world, India, Indonesia, and increasingly the West. Variations of Taarab can be found in classic, *Kidumbak* (club/ more rhythmic) and *Beni* (big band/ colonial military) styles. Taarab varies in form, contexts of performance and performers. These variations indicate that: (i) there is a high level of creolisation (localisation) and bricolage in Zanzibari music, (ii) that there are different ways in which Taarab is politicised, (iii) that there are different contexts in which meaning is conveyed through Taarab, and (iv) that Taarab produces multidirectional communication. From the point of view of ICH preservation, culture managers would need to take these variations into account and attempt to reflect these in their documentation.

Taarab was originally the preserve of the elite. It was created in Zanzibar during the reign of Seyyid Barghash (1870-88) and was a form of nineteenth century courtly praise music or poetry historically performed in Arabic for Zanzibar's sultans (Fair 2001: 171). In its classical form it is a product of the elite of Zanzibar and is associated with the urban, Arab population of the island. Instruments used in this classical Egyptian-style orchestra include: full violin section, cello and bass, accordion, oud, qanun, keyboards and ney flute. Fair says that Taarab 'remained a cultural symbol of wealth, power, and exclusiveness of the landed, slave-owning aristocracy' (Fair 2001: 173).

Attempts to popularise Taarab first occurred among musicians (especially those slave or working class, Hadhrami men) who attempted to find favour with the elite by attempting to perform Taarab. However, their music was not well received because it was deemed either to be Ngoma (drumming music common to mainland Africans), or because it was performed by low class dockworkers. In the late nineteenth century, Taarab became a part of the pastimes and politics of ex-slaves. This population sought to improve their socioeconomic position by moving to the urban areas, adopting Islam and becoming 'respectable'.

Siti Binti Saad, an ex-slave African woman, played a pivotal role in the popularisation of Taarab, an act that would also enable challenges to existing negative perceptions of the ex-slave population. Siti used Taarab as a means to reflect on issues of power, oppression and conflict on the island. She sang in Swahili not Arabic, showing that the music of the oppressors could be popularised and made relevant to whole of Zanzibar, not just those of aristocratic descent. Her band also used instruments (*Ki-dumbak* [drums], *Cherewa* [maracas] and *Sanduku* [tea-chest bass]) not common to Taarab, leading to comments that her musicians were producing a form of *ki-taarab* (little, lesser Taarab). Siti's music and life are often reflected upon in arts and cultural gatherings on the island as a way of reminding those of African descent of their beginnings, their history of oppression and their need to craft an independent identity[29] separate from the one that is 'imposed' upon them by the Tanzanian state. In 1928, Siti Binti Saad's music was recorded in Bombay and it became widely available in the region, spurring the development of this music as a form of social critique. Taarab became a means for conversation, gossip, flirtation and political commentary. For slave descendants, it also became a means of conveying meaning. In the lyrics of Siti's songs, the hardship, pain and frustration of slave descendants are vividly conveyed.

In the course of the last 60 years, Taarab has been politicised in other ways. It has offered Zanzibari women in particular a space[30] in which to speak about their lives and their experiences in a mostly conservative Muslim society. It provided many women with a socially acceptable arena where they could meet other women, share advice and have a means of entertainment.

Shortly after the Revolution, the Tanzanian state portrayed Taarab musicians and music as subversive. The Culture Music Club, a popular band on the island, was 'taken over' by the state. The band was given an ultimatum, either they played songs chosen by state apparatchiks, wore state uniforms (similar to uniforms worn by the CCM's youth brigade) and abolished anti-CCM lyrics, or they would be shut down. The Culture Music Club went along with this demand, and only recently has the club attempted to reclaim its autonomy, even reverting to the use of its original name as the Malindi (brothers who love one another) Club. Many Taarab groups decided not to sing in public in anymore and many lost their status, others simply disbanded on the basis that 'it was no fun anymore' (Fair 2001), but Taarab did not disappear and has in fact been revitalised on Zanzibar. Some see this as a sign of the growing strength of CUF on the island or that the revitalisation is a way for the island society to assert its independence and strength for the elections in 2005. Others argue (see below) that international investment in Taarab and other cultural forms in Zanzibar is having a more important impact on such music and art than state-inspired politics.

At the time of my initial research, I learned that bilateral cooperation between Tanzania, American and European donors, funded the Zanzibar International Film (and music) Festival (ZIFF). Interviews with ZIFF organisers on what the potential pitfalls of such collaboration might be suggest that external investment and promotion of culture industries is desperately needed but that there are fears about such investment shaping the art form and delivery of artists leading to the de-authentication [31] of indigenous music. Further research on the ways and extent to which external culture industries are involved in the reformulation of Taarab songs and performance is needed before a deeper discussion of this topic can take place.

However, fieldwork in Zanzibar also showed that ZIFF itself is playing a vital role in the shaping of music forms like Taarab that may ultimately influence the form of Taarab and the course of ICH preservation on the island. ZIFF produces a particular context for the exchange and expression of culture. If we look at *Kidumbak* and *Beni* forms of Taarab performance, one finds a level of spontaneity that does not usually appear in classic Taarab performance. I found myself asking if this presentation of Taarab may subvert one of its fundamental objectives, which is to produce music that is itself a form of resistance.

At the festival, I also had the sense that Taarab fostered a sense of belonging for different members of the audience. It was difficult to ascertain whether the mostly Muslim audience were keen to assert their Zanzibari identity and saw (therefore) their attendance at Taarab performances as a means of visible resistance to mainlanders. At one evening show of Taarab, it appeared that the music could be a way of 'harnessing local sentiments' (Rowlands 2002: 156) so that it could be revered (by local intellectuals and ordinary people) as a source of elite or respectable culture. This was apparent in ZIFF's description of Nadi Ikhwan Safaa (Malindi Taarab founded in 1905), as 'Taarab in its original beauty — delicate poetry, outstanding vocal performances — which revel in their elaborate ornamentation the close connection to their Arabic roots, and finely chiselled instrumentals. Love, companionship, friendship, the enjoyment of music, the pains of sadness, all find expression in the moving performances and the sweet sounds of their orchestral arrangements'. On the website, the music of Ikhwan Safaa is contrasted with and elevated over other forms of Taarab on the island, suggesting that classical Taarab is a means to anchoring Zanzibar's past in its (Arabic) glorious (but tainted) past. Michael Rowlands made a similar discovery in his ethnography on heritage in Mali and Cameroon, where he noted that culture managers themselves were deeply involved in brokerage, gate keeping *and* the assigning of meaning.

Thus at ZIFF 2004 there appeared to be several objectives and politics at play. There were for example various performers and music genres from East Africa and beyond, and it seemed to me that the choices of ZIFF organisers sought to emphasise that which is Zanzibari (including the Coconut Band who produce a fusion of Congolese rhumba and traditional Zanzibari music); that which is accepted by the Tanzanian state (the JKU Steel Band and Diamond Modern Taarab), and that which is indicative of political liberation and change. One of the East African singers chosen to perform at ZIFF, Achien'g Abura from Kenya, is a singer, pianist and composer. She has an academic background in environment and conflict management and is a strong advocate for social transformation in Kenya. ZIFF also hosted the Palestinian singer, Arnus Markal, described as a 'Christian and Communist', who sings in Arabic and infuses her lyrics with poetry and protest. Bongo Maffin from South Africa also performed at the festival and are described on ZIFF's website as 'the sound of the first generation of South Africans unshackled from the yoke of apartheid' (www.ziff.org). In Zanzibari music there were attempts to infuse lyrics with the *Rusha Roho* (risqué) style that is generally found in the traditional *Kidumabaki* (small club band).

The 'collapse' of the socialist state of Tanzania has created new uncertainties and opportunities that complicate local politics and the process of culture management. With the fall of socialism and the re-introduction of capitalism one finds that Taarab performers and other musicians' forms in Zanzibar are able to draw upon range of genres and politics beyond Zanzibar to configure their music. This process (as I have argued elsewhere) is assisted by what some Zanzibari's call 'cool politics', cooperative strategies encouraged by experiences borne of Monsoon trade that compelled people of the Indian Ocean to accommodate difference.

The examples presented above show that there is a politics (as Askew and Fair argue) largely 'external' to Taarab itself that imbue the music with meaning. This politics is further diversified in the variation of performers, contexts and instruments used to perform Taarab. From this perspective, Taarab achieves multidirectional communication but also serves as a point of conversion for the differently categorised groups on the island. However, at the end of my brief stay in Zanzibar, I found myself asking whether there was deeper meaning in Taarab (particularly informal performances at home and weddings) that performers attempted to communicate with their audiences.

The deeper politics of Taarab presents specific challenges to those concerned with the preservation of intangible heritage in the Indian Ocean region. UNESCO perceives intangible cultural resources as a means to preserve human diversity (in the face of modernisation and Western globalisation) and to ensure sustainable development. But can and should diversity be preserved? In Zanzibar, diversification is an ongoing process contributing to the hybridisation of culture and identity.

A closer look at Taarab in Zanzibar suggests that this is a cultural form that has been shaped by many different political forces. Which version will the culture managers preserve? What are the implications of ignoring variations of Taarab? And if Taarab is not chosen at all as a resource that can and should be preserved (perhaps because it is originally the music of oppressors), what are the implications for the preservation of Zanzibari heritage? It is true that because of the diverse experience of cultural exchange, Zanzibari 'heritage' exists between groups as part of social process rather than being a 'gift', and it is informed by violence and globalisation. It is, in my view, important to take these factors into account, especially the ways in which Zanzibaris have dealt with their experience of these social forces. However, as the Mauritius data shows, we also need to reflect on the music form itself. How is the music produced? How is it documented? What contexts allow for particular kinds of performance? What do these different contexts mean for those who are part of the audience? Being able to answer these questions would help culture managers to question not only their choices in heritage preservation but also enable them to critically reflect on challenges to identification, curating and the communication of 'heritage'.

Attempting to see what lies behind the lyrics helped to reveal that slave descendant communities in the southwest Indian Ocean have developed ways to encounter their history of violence and oppression. Presently, in Zanzibar, the commercialisation of music means that some of these rich knowledge sources and cultural strategies are being glossed over or repackaged for a commercially-oriented international market, and that this is happening at a time when these unique social forms and ideas have not even been documented. Broader politics affecting these local cultural forms are apparent (for example) in the largely Western-inspired regimes of heritage preservation, which seem to be diminishing the very things that they wish to conserve. In the case of Taarab we find that spontaneous composition led to memorised verses, and the people who produce these are needed for the achievement of 'authentic' cultural reproduction. How might preservation occur with these factors in place? Indeed, UNESCO has realised the importance of a 'work's faithfulness to itself, its origins and environment'[32] but how this will be achieved where there are divergent paradigms of communication, restitution and management remains to be seen. Perhaps closer attention to the frameworks and meaning that people themselves produce from their experience might be a place to start. Spending time in Stone Town at the start of the research, I focused on institutions and their role in training and managing heritage.

ZIFF and ICH

ZIFF is increasingly playing a vital role in defining ICH in Zanzibar, particularly by fostering conditions for the exchange and expression of culture. At ZIFF 2004, there were various performers and music genres from East Africa and beyond, and seemed to me that ZIFF sought to energise political and artistic autonomy. Speaking about ZIFF, Imruh said that the internationalisation of the festival is finally de-mystifying Zanzibar and is putting its rituals, art and music on a global stage. This is allowing Zanzibari artists who fear for their safety and their creative freedom to have another space in which to produce their music. The 'collapse' of the socialist state of Tanzania has also created new uncertainties and opportunities, allowing residents to take risks that they otherwise would not have a few years ago. With the fall of socialism and the re-introduction of capitalism one finds that Taarab performers and other musicians forms in Zanzibar are able to draw upon range of genres and politics beyond Zanzibar to configure their music. 'This', Imruh argued, 'is a good thing. It promotes "cool politics", a politics of tolerance and openness. It's the kind of thing that has existed in this place for a long time but has not always been able to come out into the open. It reminds me of another older kind of globalisation. A globalisation that is not new to this part of the world'.

For Imruh, 'cool' politics is a historical and contemporary response to violence and oppression. It is also a means to accommodate and meld various cultural forms and modes of cultural transfer in a particular form of music or oral history. This encourages social openness and tolerance in a society where there is a long experience of social and racial segregation, but it also offers a means to resist and defy oppression. In this context, music forms and oral histories do not really belong to any particular group. The boundaries of the cultural form are hazy and the form itself is porous and changing. Furthermore, the cultural forms are embedded in a context where there are morally contradictory heritages. The close symbiosis between morally affirming and 'destructive' heritage poses all kinds of problems for culture managers who seek to identify particular cultural forms for preservation and documentation. Towards the end of my initial fieldwork in Zanzibar, I noticed the growing presence of more conventional forms of globalisation and its homogenising effects.

One afternoon, I walked to the garden court of the House of Wonders so that I could see a theatrical re-enactment of Siti Binti Saad's life. The performance was in English and Swahili, the audience a pitiful clutch of foreigners with exception to those half-hanging from the windows in a building facing the garden. The play was entitled 'Bringing the Past Alive', and featured a young, beautiful woman who portrayed Siti's rise from the ranks as a slave descendant to a celebrated member of Zanzibari society. It was difficult to hear what the actress was saying. Her voice was drowned out by the Congolese music across the road in Forodhani gardens. After the play had ended, I went to the Congolese performance. On stage there were two men gyrating to the music (Zanzibar is Islamic so women are not allowed to dance in public) and the gardens were so full of people that I could not find a space closer to the stage. This experience made me wonder about the extent to which Zanzibaris are really concerned with heritage preservation, (especially in the form dictated by heritage regimes), and whether many would perhaps prefer Western globalisation.

Rosabelle Boswell

Conclusion

Recent publications to be found in *Anthropology News* 44: 9, (December 2003), *Cultural Anthropology* (CA Forum, February 2002) and *Museum International: Views and Visions of the Intangible* (no. 221, 2004) offer contemporary discussions of ICH and the practical aspects of its management. These have raised questions about the politics of ICH management (see Goody 2004; Kirshenblatt-Gimblet 2004; van Zanten 2004 and Wendland 2004). Arizpe's (2004) and Nettleford's (2004) papers on ICH in a rapidly changing global context support these politically oriented debates. Resources that also reflect on the political dimensions of heritage resource identification and management (Ost 2001 and Radice 2003), also provide a starting point for my thoughts on ICH in the Indian Ocean. In this chapter, I have attempted to show that while such debates are vital for an understanding of ICH and its management in Zanzibar, we also need to consider locally generated debates on heritage and the particular politics that inform these.

The growing significance of tourism to economic development in the southwest Indian Ocean region also calls for an economically oriented discussion of ICH initiatives. Tourism's effects on society in Asia and the Caribbean are plentiful (McElroy 2000, Cohen 1982, Garrod and Fyall 2000, Pattullo 1996), and point to the significance of this industry to production (and de-authentication) of culture on a mass scale. In the Indian Ocean region, states only seem to see the economic dimensions and potential of tourism (see Lutz 1994 and Ghosh, Siddique and Gabbay 2003). If the latter view prevails, what impact will private and state tourism objectives have on ICH preservation in the Indian Ocean? This is too much of an important question to be left unanswered. Research in Mauritius (March-April 2004) and Seychelles (June 2005) shows that the government has been quick to identify tangible heritage sites as they are easier to 'package' and market in a global tourist market. So far, there have been no attempts to settle on and identify intangible heritage even though the director general of UNESCO visited the island and formally encouraged Mauritius (in February 2004) not only to ratify the ICH convention but also to begin the process of ICH identification. It would seem to me that similar kinds of problems (issues of representation, the delicate balance of politics in a multiethnic society and the fact of hybridisation) might influence Zanzibari cultural managers' responses to ICH preservation and management.

Islanders of the Indian Ocean are today part of a world in which there are new uncertainties, inequalities and opportunities. My thoughts about Zanzibar society suggest that non-western forces (not necessarily oriental) of globalisation heavily influence the particular ideas, forms and experiences of heritage in these societies. However, I also see that contemporary factors (for example, violence perpetrated by the modern state) have an effect on approaches to and definitions of heritage. These have important implications for the contemporary management of cultural heritage in Zanzibar. For one, heritage in Zanzibar is more than a stable 'gift' from the past. In this context, heritage is a precarious and continually generating identity that is inspired and sustained by disruptive forces and experiences.

Further along in the course of research in Zanzibar, I would like to research various local cultural expressions. This will require more extensive participant-observation and interviewing beyond Stone Town and the institutions involved in heritage management. I suspect that this will reveal that cultural forms pegged as heritage do not simply exist for cultural regeneration and reinforcement. But that they also offer an alternative epistemic framework, a means to actualise alternative political spaces and a different form of belonging in an increasingly homogenised world.

7. Socialism and Change: Seychelles

The following chapter offers a discussion of anthropological data collected in Seychelles in June 2005. The chapter is divided into three parts. The first introduces Seychelles and the social factors influencing cultural interaction. The second part deals explicitly with institutional challenges to heritage management, and the third part offers some insight into occupation diversity as a form of cultural and industrial heritage in Mahé. Based on the perceived importance of intangible culture to identity and economy in the Seychelles, the report concludes that further investment in intangible heritage projects is required from the private sector and government.

The Seychelles is emerging from almost two decades of socialist rule, is relatively homogeneous, and regionally less economically influential than Mauritius. The Seychelles also have long histories of oppression and currently seek a higher level of inclusion in international society. In the archipelago decisions about what and whose heritage to preserve, whether the heritage will be of universal value (and therefore worthy of inscription on the WHL), the extent to which certain heritage should be preserved, are heavily influenced by social and not simply material considerations. How do countries like the Seychelles reconcile the seemingly contradictory requirement of being their 'true selves' and producing a product for wealthy and powerful international counterparts?

Heritage Issues and Management in the Seychelles

My first encounter with the Seychelles occurred before I arrived on the islands in June 2005. I was informed by one of my project advisors that I should avoid going there because the state officials were not in favour of independent research. The advisor said that she had experienced many problems in attempting to take research materials back home and that she had been accused of copyright infringement. Each researcher coming to the Seychelles has to sign an 'agreement' or research contract with the state in which the researcher has to identify her research topic, location of research, contacts in the 'field', residential address and the duration of the research.

The National Heritage Division informed me that the agreement is a formal, government document which aims to protect local resources from being exploited by external interests. The document had come into being shortly after the Seychelles became a socialist state in 1977. The then newly elected cabinet emphasised the documentation and preservation of popular heritage resources as a way to achieve a more equitable society. For until then, British and French history, artefacts, languages and places of interest dominated the social scene. The research contract included a number of clauses which (to me) appeared to protect the interests of the Seychellois. However, the advisor was deeply concerned about statements aimed at curtailing her autonomy. In the contract, the heritage division is given the right to 'monitor the research work of [the researcher] in the Republic of the Seychelles ... to cease any collaboration with [the researcher] if the end use of the final report will have a damaging effect on the image and the reputation of any individuals in the Republic of Seychelles' (*Draft Research Agreement* June 2005). The contract also states that 'The Seychellois community (informants) reserves their constitutional right not to provide information to [the researcher] if they are not comfortable with any part of the exchange'.

Although aware of potential problems that I might encounter once there, I decided to take a chance. I felt that I would be in a better position than my advisor because I spoke *Kreol* (the lingua franca of the islands) and had lived in an autocratic state. I believed that I would be more sensitive to the nuances of local experience and would be more likely to perceive the ambiguities of living in a pro-socialist state. Being from Mauritius, I was also sensitive to the vulnerability of small island states to the precarious tourism industry. I accepted that they have the right to protect their country from unnecessarily negative publicity. Although my first encounter with the National Heritage Division was awkward (I was not accustomed to signing 'limiting' research contracts), I found that ultimately, the Division did assist me in my research and that the research contract was not simply a piece of 'red tape'. It was also an important source of information in terms of what local professionals thought of their heritage. For them, they had inalienable rights to it and were entitled to protect it from exploitation.

Managing Heritage in the Seychelles

Gabriel Essack, the principal research officer at the National Heritage Division, met me at the Victoria bus station. He offered to take me to NHD office, *La Bastille*, and wasted no time in telling me about the researcher who wanted to 'come and take our resources without acknowledging us for it'. He related the story of other researchers who had come to neighbouring islands at the expense of the government in 2001 and had failed to supply them with any report of their findings. He argued that such events promote a negative image of the Division and of government to the citizens of the Seychelles, as it signals the misuse of public funds. 'If we are to do this properly', he said, 'we need to make sure that each researcher coming here signs an agreement which also suits our needs'. Shortly after, I was taken to 'present my credentials' to the director-general for heritage, Marie-France McGregor. She asked if I could speak *Kreol*, and I answered that I did. This seemed to break the ice and I went on (in *Kreol*) to discuss my research plans before signing the agreement. Both McGregor and Essack seemed happy with my choice; documenting occupational diversity was a topic of relevance to the Seychelles, where people had survived because they had developed a myriad of subsistence skills over the centuries.

The heritage office focuses on three key areas: Anthropology/oral tradition; monuments and artefacts; copyright and the protection of heritage. The oral tradition unit concentrates on the documentation and preservation of stories/ folklore, music and indigenous healing practices. In terms of tangible heritage management, the officers focus on site identification and maintenance. In recent years, many different sites (graveyards, bridges, sites of communal work) have been identified, restored and written about in the NHD's newsletters. The broad programme of the office is to disseminate information on culture and cultural activities, manage cultural sites, network and gain information from or exchange information with, experts in the field of heritage and train novices to do research on heritage. In 2005, the division received sufficient funds from the government to carry out its activities. Government disbursed approximately 500,000 Seychellois Rupees for site management alone.

The division does, according to Essack, face many problems in executing its duties. Its current personnel lack the level of training necessary to carry out research and to write about heritage in a meaningful way. Public perception of culture is also a challenge. Government officials do not always understand the arguments made by culture experts; trained in political 'science' or economics they fail to see the utility of culture in the development of the country. In Essack's view, the office also lacks knowledge about the process of heritage preservation. In short, more qualified personnel are required to run the office and a better organisational plan may be needed. In the archival room for example, primary documentation lay in disarray and the room was too small for the protection and classification of these vital cultural resources. However, Essack was also focused on the restoration of the built environment. Although the archives housed many documents indicating Seychellois' high esteem for, and concern with intangible heritage, this did not seem to receive appropriate attention.

Occupation Diversity

Over the past two decades, the Marxist tradition has been criticised for its presentation of human labour in purely instrumental terms. 'Labour is, in the first place, a process in which both man and nature participate, and in which man of his own accord starts, regulates, and controls the material re-actions between himself and nature' (Marx 1967: 177). Critiques of the materialist approach in the work of Arendt (1958), Habermas (1975) and Wallman (1979), indicate an important distinction between labour and work. While labour concerns the 'metabolic exchange with nature' (Arendt 1958 cited in Ulin 2002: 693), work is a social process that has culturally formative potential. Work involves social interaction. It is also part of cultural production and produces identity. In Jiménez's discussion of work and personhood, he adds that 'work is a refraction of other social processes—a means by which people rescale their sense of self and otherness' (2003: 14). Recent postcolonial studies of identity (Abebe 2001; Comaroff 2001) however, caution against seeing any particular social process as being 'responsible' for the formation of identity. In the Seychelles, I found that work is indeed a social process. It was and is still fundamental to cultural and identity production. To this end, I felt it necessary to highlight not just the forms of work but also work flexibility and occupation diversity as important forms of cultural heritage in the islands.

In the course of research, I found that for many generations the Seychellois had taken on a diversity of occupations. The fact of living in a small island society with few skilled individuals meant that local inhabitants were compelled to multi-task. In the time of French and then British colonial rule, the situation of black Seychellois required families to learn about and develop many skills. Oral history records available at the NHD research room note that the average day of the plantation worker was divided into early morning plantation (cultivation and herding) work and late afternoon fishing, planting, hunting and repair work. A barter system prevailed where villagers exchanged animals (pigs, chickens) for agricultural produce or services such as child and health care. In 1977 with the advent of a socialist government, things changed. Citizens were discouraged from starting their own businesses, the state became the major employer and the population became largely dependent on state support and financing.

In May 2005, it was noted in *The Nation* (the Seychelles national newspaper) that 'entrepreneurs no have access to Rs10,000 (ten thousand Seychellois Rupees) from the Young Enterprise Scheme (YES) to purchase basic equipment or materials for the development of a cottage industry'. There is also the possibility for entrepreneurs to take out loans of Rs50,000 at a low interest rate (one percent) for further development. Cottage industries do not need licences to sell their products and were initially advised to make use of local shops for the distribution of their goods. On May 1 2005, the Seychelles Small Enterprise Promotion Agency (SEnPA) began to administer the registration, promotion and management of these small industries. A basic rule is that each industry cannot employ more than five Seychellois at a time and their sales revenue cannot exceed Rs800,000 per annum; 'only light activities are allowed, such as art, handicraft, small scale manufacturing, agro-processing, basic equipment repair and maintenance, child-minding, food- processing and textiles' (*The Nation*, vol xxviii, No. 82, 3 May, 2005: p. 2).

The reason for encouraging the development of cottage industries is that the Seychellois can begin to participate in the privatisation process in a more inclusive manner. State-run operations can no longer absorb the flood of new workers coming onto the job market every year. To this end, SEnPA is offering training to young entrepreneurs to help them manage their newly established businesses. The government predicts that the 300 cottage industries financed since 2004 will contribute to approximately Rs12 million to the islands' GDP per annum. Already, Rs6 million has been invested in these industries and over 342 new jobs have been created (*The Nation*, vol xxviii, No. 82, 3 May, 2005: pp. 1-2). The encouragement of cottage industries is partly motivated by the demand for employment in the country and the fact that Seychelles does have a significant debt burden. The recent visit of the World Bank Country Director for Seychelles, James Bond, indicates that while the Bank supports the important economic changes made in the islands, more should be done about the country's debt burden and the role of the government in the economy. The director stated that there is 'a need to adjust to a new role model. That model will inevitably have a smaller role for government in the production sector, perhaps a larger role in the maintaining investment in people, making sure that the economy functions efficiently' (Ibid).

Halfway through my stay in the Seychelles, I identified the southern village of Takamaka as a potential site for research on the issue of occupation diversity. Material from the NHD research archives showed many pictures of different work activities in Takamaka. Conversations with locals in around the area of Anse La Mouche (the east coast settlement where I was staying) indicated that

Takamaka was still 'fairly traditional'. The southern part of Mahé island is relatively undeveloped compared to the northern region and so I thought that the islanders living there might have conserved some of the occupations that I had read about in the archival documents.

Takamaka

Takamaka is a coastal village backed by steep granite slopes. It has the obligatory church, corner stores and social centre office to be found in any small village in Mahé. The day I arrived there, it had been raining heavily. Leaves, tree trunks and other debris blocked the roads into the village. I had managed to secure the help of a local social services representative and she offered to take me to my first interviewee, Mrs Pothen. This interviewee told me that she has family in France and La Reunion (sister island to Mauritius) and that although she does not know them personally, she knows that they are from *grand familles* (important, noble families).[33] She left school at the age of fourteen and began to sew for a living. Looking back on her families' past, she clearly remembers that her father did everything—carpentry, working on the plantation, looking after his own garden and selling manioc to the villagers. This was a necessity because there were twelve children in the house.

Reflecting on her experiences of the sewing business, the interviewee noted that it was not always easy to run one's own business. Even though the prices are low, there are many people who simply cannot afford to pay for the clothing they have ordered her to sew. Fabric has to be bought overseas with foreign exchange as there are few suppliers on Mahé and one can only gain access for foreign currency once one has registered with SEnPA. At the Pothen's house, one of the younger daughters was at home. She had a baby but also formally unemployed. I asked whether she would like to join her mother as a seamstress or do something similar for a 'job'. She was not keen to do this, wanting to work as a receptionist in town rather than owning her own business.

Another young interviewee (outside the Pothen household) Marilyne, was also asked about her future plans. The 17 year old had just ended her school career. She was not keen to return to or pursue further education even though she had the opportunity and finances made available to her to do so. I asked her whether she had ever thought of starting her own small business. She answered that she was looking forward to starting a job in an office 'somewhere' but did not see herself as a potential business person or cottage industry owner.

Retrospective interviews in Takamaka with Mirna Vidot, Olga Des Aubins, Marguerite Marie-Joseph and Flora Seth revealed that in the past many villagers of Takamaka were actively involved in producing their own livelihoods. Olga Des Aubins told me that in the past, it was easy to get straw from the latanier tree. She was born in Takamaka in a family of nine children (six girls and three boys). At the time of the interview, she was 71 years old. During World War Two, there was very little access to fabric and shoes and other clothing. She clearly remembers taking her First Holy Communion without shoes, and that in those days, many of the inhabitants wore dresses made from the same fabric. Nevertheless women and girls were prolific hat weavers and basket makers. Olga told me the following:

> My father was a carpenter. On weekends he would go fishing so that we would have enough 'meat' for the week. On the days that he managed to get a pig, we roasted parts of it and salted other bits so that there would be enough for the really difficult times. My mother on the other hand, stayed at home to look after us. Even so, she embroidered fabric and wove hats, baskets and other beautiful things. My husband was in the War and fought for the English in Cairo, Egypt. But when he came back, he started his garden and spent quite a lot of time fishing. We travelled to Anse Royale [an east coast village on Mahé] to buy fabric and I kept the family income going by sewing brassieres and other underwear. I also spent a lot of time braiding straw to sell it to weavers and sometimes made hats and bags.

In those days she said, '*nou ti vive dans marmitte camarade aujourd'hui nou tous alle la boutik.*' 'We lived in one another's casserole, now we all go to the shops'. In other words, we no longer rely on each other. She also went on to say that 'now that I am "retired", I spend my days child-minding basically looking after my grand-children'. As far as she was aware, there were no crèches in Takamaka, mothers have to take their children to Anse Royale.

Similar accounts of occupation diversity were reported by Mirna Vidot. This 67 year old mother and grandmother told me that when her father left the family (she was only four years old at the time), her mother did all kinds of jobs to keep them alive. There were six children in the house at the time, three boys and three girls. When she was small, the family lived in a thatched house in Quatre-Bornes. There were wooden planks on the floor and walls, three bedrooms and a small verandah. There were not many people living there because it was so high up in the mountains. Nevertheless, they were not isolated. Her mother had people come up to the house to fix bamboo into a water pipe that ran from a nearby river directly to their house. A system of exchange prevailed and people shared their skills and resources as a way of surviving. What she remembers clearly is the extent to which local families participated in savings schemes and associations which aimed to provide entertainment in the village of Takamaka. Musicians in the village were paid for their services from the associations' savings and parents would accompany their children to these *Balles invitées*. '*Sa'*, Mirna said, '*ti gou!*' (Those were fantastic!). Those coming to the party would bring some goods, drink, food and other perceived necessities. Girls in her family would, for example, help the host to clean the house the morning after the party had finished. Even the storyteller in their midst would be recompensed for his 'duties' with the appropriate 'payment'. In some cases, this would be an appropriately timed bottle of *kalou* [a locally brewed alcoholic drink].

My interview with Flora Seth revealed a different story. Arriving in the Seychelles in the early 1970s from Kenya, Flora began to work as a waitress in one of the newly established hotels on the island. Since then, she has always worked in hotels and has never thought to look for an alternative or multiple source of income. Flora and I spoke English to each other rather than Kreol. She had not spoken in English for more than ten years when I met her and longed for the life she had with her parents in Mombasa. As an immigrant it had taken many years for Flora to adjust to life in the Seychelles. Although the inhabitants can speak English she was not made to feel a part of social networks (especially in the early days) because she could not speak Kreol. Flora also had a very troubled relationship with her former husband and told me that she felt the Seychellois are extremely patriarchal: 'Women do not own much, they do not control much either'. In cases such as Flora, one has to examine the experiences of recent generations to ascertain why there is not such enthusiasm for multiple occupations, or for owning one's own business. Indeed the recent legacy of socialism has impacted on peoples' perceptions of their capacities and initiative. But careful attention (and further research) is also needed into the lack of leadership opportunities (and ownership opportunities) offered to the local Seychellois in the time of slavery and colonialism. Is it possible that these long-term legacies of subordination continue to impact on the ways in which the Seychellois see themselves as participants in their economy?

The multitasking of earlier generations of Seychellois is also confirmed in documented oral histories. The 83 year old Felix Joliecoeur of Kazern (Plaisance, Mahé) noted in 1983 and 1985 that in Kazern, 'mon plant mayok, mon plant patat, mon plant legim mon plant kanbar, mon plant ziromon...patol, papay... pistas...tou sa ki mon gannyen...k'man mon fini travay laba mon al lapes' (*Lesperyans II* A/10.12 pp. 29-65).[34] Olive Nicole, a 75 year old resident of La

Digue in 1980, emphasised the importance of exchange to the management of multiple livelihoods. He said, 'le ou pou desann ou, mon a donn ou en pti koson, mon a donn ou de poules ... tantot lernou'n fini dinen I apel tou sa wazen nou assize la nou a vini sakenn eke nm ti lasyet. I koup en morso dimyel...sa wazen ki la antre nou an sosyete, nou a manze nou a vant I a plen.' (p. 5).[35]

Conclusion

The research data presented above clearly show that a long tradition of occupation diversity exists in the Seychelles and that this is not just for instrumental purposes. Work in the Seychelles informed and continues to inform local identity and culture. In the past, it was through 'apprenticeships' that young people came to learn of basket and fish-trap weaving, sewing, cooking, planting and music making. These activities occurred in socially and culturally significant spaces. They also engendered culturally and politically significant relationships and shaped social interactions and communications in the domestic sphere. The shift from work on the plantations, for instance, indicated a temporary release from the control and direction of the overseer. Once at the beach, fishermen worked cooperatively, employing their cumulative knowledge in fixing nets and traps and in judging the best times to set out to sea.

Interviews with younger residence in Mahé in June 2005 indicated that many are keen to be employed rather than seeking to start their own businesses. This shift in interest suggests that young Seychellois are firmly anchoring their identity and dignity in a 'new' globalising economy. Past means of survival, meaning and economy are today, not regarded highly. This is a great pity because it is the very flexibility and socially embedded society that enabled older generations of Seychellois to navigate the difficult times of global integration. As the society becomes more atomised and industrialised, it seems that more Seychellois are keen to have access to and consume goods that are produced on the global market. While it is important to recognise that the islands are now part of a globalised economy, it is also important to negotiate the terms of inclusion into a globalised economy. One way of attempting to reduce the negative consequences of globalisation is to ensure that the local population is able to produce sustainable livelihoods which can be useful in international trade. In view of UNESCO's emphasis on heritage preservation and management, it seems that now is a good time to look at how heritage and particularly occupation diversity, which is (as I saw it), an emic expression of heritage on the islands, can be married to economic growth and development. Presently, the National Heritage Division appears to be concerned with the preservation of the built environment. Conversations with the heritage managers suggest that this is largely because the public and government do not really appreciate arguments for the preservation of intangible heritage. In short, there is 'no site' to preserved, publicised or 'useful' for tourism purposes. Government is therefore more likely to disburse funds for the preservation of monuments and tangible heritage.

8. Conclusions

Doing research in Mauritius, Zanzibar and Seychelles and participating in the 29th Session of the World Heritage Committee Meeting (July 2005) has encouraged me to question the values underlying the 'Western' heritage management ethos and the 'openness' of the West to alternative interpretations of heritage. Encounters in the field also encouraged me to question whether the adoption of contemporary heritage practices by local people reflects a conscious engagement with those values in terms of their own priorities and interests. Critical reflection on dominant interpretations of heritage is important to African countries. Not only does it reveal 'received wisdom' about the concept and underlying motivations in the implementation of heritage initiatives, it has major implications for the sustainable development of Africa and her people.

Ethnographic research in the three above-mentioned island societies clearly reveals the extent to which 'heritage is an unequally distributed and appropriated gift', continually constructed by the rich and powerful, but also subject to contestations by the poor and marginal. In Mauritius the island nation's image is paramount to its success in attracting sufficient foreign investment. There is (as I discovered there), a concerted effort to present homogeneous ethnic identities to satisfy the intenational tourist in search of 'packaged' identity for a package holiday. In Zanzibar, past interethnic violence is making it difficult for local inhabitants to motivate for conservation efforts of the built environment. The persistent division (not readily articulated in the presence of strangers), between Africans and the descendants of Arabs is complicating the process of heritage identification. It may well have negative implications for the nomination and inscription process. Readings of religious life in Zanzibar (Parkin 2001) indicate that the islands have hybrid intangible heritages that are not easily articulated in a modernising nation-state. Specific references to spirit possession for instance (particularly during the 1995 national elections), suggest that Zanzibaris have important cosmological ideas and that these do not 'sit well' with contemporary (Western) notions of heritage. In the Seychelles, there exists a window of opportunity for an inclusive and emic expression of ICH. The country is in the process of transition from socialism to democracy. High value is placed on local expressions of culture and heritage managers are open to suggestions in terms of the identification of ICH and its management. At the end of my research, it was unclear whether the Seychelles would take this important opportunity to adequately address issues of heritage and sustainable development, or whether it would go the Mauritius route, specifically whether the Seychellois would advocate a continued focus on the development of tangible heritage in the hope of diversifying its tourism sector in oder to secure foreign investment.

The broad conclusions are as follows:

- There are broader historical factors such as trade, slavery and globalisation that influence the form and experience of ICH in the chosen research sites.

- The islands are part of important overlapping zones. These zones are created by trade, religion, slavery and ethnicity. Each island has experienced these to varying degrees and they impact on what the islanders consider as their tangible and intangible heritage.

These social forces have also produced unintended or forms of heritage that may be morally ambiguous (such as violence and commercialism) or rarely reflected (such as fragrance, see Boswell forthcoming 2008) in the West.

- Heritage regimes currently impose various logistical, political and ideological constraints on heritage identification and management in these societies. These do not assist in the democratisation process and do not allow for the sustainable management of heritage. This was evident in the Mauritius case study, where experts were called in to assess the heritage value of Le Morne without a careful consideration of local perspectives and cultural needs.

The island societies also produce their own epistemologies and modes of cultural communication and transfer. These, I argue, form a vital part of their heritage and are the most difficult to conserve or manage.

- Theoretically, we need to develop emic analytical frameworks so that we can understand and know the better ways of dealing with ICH. Can all heritage be managed? Is the 'preservation' of diversity possible or desirable?

- The ICH of these islands indicates ways in which various groups have managed to coexist in multicultural settings. They also clearly show the extent to which developing states have to go in order to secure a measure of national dignity and material investment from the West.

Rosabelle Boswell

This research on challenges to the management of ICH in the Indian Ocean region reveals that alternative political spaces exist in these island societies. In some cases it revealed that ICH is a shared cultural resource that does not necessarily 'belong' to a particular ethnic group. In ethnically conscious societies, where the leadership emphasises pluralism, this is very difficult to accept. Whose heritage is it? Who has the authority to decide which parts of it are to be preserved and how it should be preserved and managed? In the case of Zanzibar for instance, Taarab is a popular music form that bridges the African/Arab divide.

Ethnography in these island societies also shows that ICH produces divergent modes of cultural communication and modes of cultural transfer. Heritage regimes tend to produce particular frameworks and practices for the management of tangible heritage. UNESCO has, for example, protocols regarding the preservation and communication of heritage. Diverse ways of communicating ICH (which is often dependent on tangible heritage), makes it hard for heritage managers to meet standards for the preservation/management of ICH. The data presented here clearly indicate that processes and frameworks for heritage management have to be decentralised. In view of the Africa 2009 initiative, it is important not only to educate and finance heritage managers and educators in Africa. It is necessary to create conditions that allow these managers to shape the frameworks, to identify their own policies with regard to ICH, and to offer greater flexibility in the management of funds received from UNESCO for heritage management.

The anthropological data also show that ICH is not just about the preservation of cultural resources for humanity as a whole. Viewed from the political angle, the decentralisation of heritage management will allow for the forging of stable democracies and democratic reform. It is also vital for the identity and dignity of the people in whose country the heritage resides. Furthermore the management of cultural heritage, is not just about securing foreign investment and participating in international society. It also impacts local conceptualisations of citizenship, history and identity. At a broader (and perhaps more fundamental level), heritage is central to the development of alternative epistemologies or knowledge systems. In these island societies and other parts of the developing world, the expression and validation of alternative epistemologies is imperative for true and sustainable emancipation.

Notes

1. Negative means of control might include the enactment of severely restrictive immigration laws, xenophobia or genocide.

2. 'Tanzania is one of the poorest countries in the world. The economy depends heavily on agriculture, which accounts for about half of GDP, provides 85% of exports, and employs 80% of the work force. Topography and climatic conditions, however, limit cultivated crops to only 4% of the land area. Growth in 1991-2002 featured a pickup in industrial production and a substantial increase in output of minerals, led by gold. Oil and gas exploration and development played an important role in this growth. Recent banking reforms have helped increase private sector growth and investment. Continued donor assistance and solid macroeconomic policies supported real GDP growth of more than 5.2% in 2004.' *World Factbook 2004.*

3. http://www.inadev.org/profile-tanzania.htm.

4. These manuscripts contain Arabic literature and rhetoric and are indispensable to studies of the history of ideas, diseases, treatments, witchcraft, astronomy, navigation, slavery, poetry and art of eastern Africa.

5. Cloves were first introduced to Zanzibar from Madagascar in 1818.

6. At the height of the slave trade more than 60,000 people were transported annually from the mainland to Zanzibar and from there sent to other markets in Arabia, the Indian Ocean and America. The sultan received a tax on every sale. Tippu Tip, the servant of the sultan and historically a famous slave trader on the east African coast is said to have owned more than 700 plantations by the time he died in 1905.

7. More than ninety years after the American abolition of slavery (1804) and 60 years after abolition in Mauritius (1835).

8. See Askew 2002 for a detailed discussion.

9. *The Rough Guide to Zanzibar* (Finke 2002: 41.)

10. For example, Alpers, E. 1999, 'Becoming "Mozambique": diaspora and identity in Mauritius'. Paper presented at the 160th anniversary of the abolition of apprenticeship. Réduit: University of Mauritius, In E. Alpers and V. Teelock, eds., 2001, *History, Memory and Identity*, Bell Village, Port Louis: Nelson Mandela Centre for African Culture.

11. The equivalent of the sega in Mauritius.

12. Sometimes sold, for example one was sold to the writer, Wilbur Smith.

13. See Eriksen, T. H. 1998.*Common Denominators: Ethnicity, Nation-Building and Compromise in Mauritius*. Oxford: Berg.

14. See Laville, R. 2000. 'In the politics of the rainbow: Creoles and civil society in Mauritius', *Journal of Contemporary African Studies*, 18 (2): 277-94.

15. This I have already found in the consideration of the Mauritian Sega, a popular music form initiated by Mauritian slave descendants. The lyrics and performance of the Sega contain elements that might be considered 'disrespectful' as some Segas contains sexual innuendo, political criticism and references to what might be seen as immoral behaviour.

16. A version of this chapter is published in the *Journal of Southern African Studies*, 31 (2), June 2005: 283-97.

17. Can you eat heritage?

18. I would sleep with my eyes open.

19. Local restaurants.

20. Molluscs.

21. *Ton* Michel is folklorised in a tale by Rajesh Ramdoyal (1979). *Tales from Mauritius*. London: Macmillan. And until I met him personally I had thought that he was a figment of the author's imagination.

22. Mountain.

23. Little.

24. 'We must also play the political game'.

25. 'The past is not dead. It has not even passed' (Toni Morisson, Love).

26. The organisations involved in cultural management in Zanzibar include the Stone Town Conservation and Development Authority (STCDA), Aga Khan Trust for Culture, the Zanzibar National Archives, Zanzibar International Film Festival (ZIFF) and the non-governmental organisation on the east coast

of the island, Eco+Culture. I will need to do more research on the issue of cultural management in concert with these institutions.

27. www.unesco.org/culture/industries/html.

28. In the Ngoma tradition for example, there are drumming performances by men (Kyaso), women (Ndege female initiation ritual) and drumming styles that originate on the continent, such as the Kilua (spirit evoking music and dance) from the Democratic Republic of Congo.

29. After the abolition of slavery, the continued and brutal impact of colonisation encouraged the Zanzibaris (especially those of slave descent) to work together against oppressive conditions and to devise new spaces for their autonomy. Colonial demands for hut taxes and ground rents (in urban Zanzibar where people felt that they owned land), led to unified mass action and the ground rent strikes of the late 1890s. The strikes helped people of African descent to craft a shared identity and sense of unity.

30. Another way in which Zanzibari women have been able to express their emotions and character is through dress. Their brightly printed Kangas have Kiswahili proverbs on them that enable them to say something without verbalising this in difficult social contexts. For example, some women might wear a kanga with the words: 'chongeni sana mtajiju' (say what you like, I don't give a damn) in the company of difficult in-laws or jealous friends. See Boswell 2006.

31. Authenticity being important to the goals of UNESCO's ICH preservation programme.

32. www.unesco.org/culture/industries/html.

33. I intend to write a longer piece on the settler families and identity in Seychelles. Mrs Pothen and a few others interviewed thus far form an integral part of the settler community on Mahé.

34. 'I planted manioc, potatoes, pumpkin, pawpaw, peanuts...everything I could ... When I was done with that, I went fishing.'

35. 'When you "come down" [come to my house], I will give you a small pig or some chickens ... at night after I have finished dinner I call my neighbours, they each bring a small plate, we sit down and I "cut" a piece of honey comb, we share it and we become part of a society [group] and we eat until we are full'.

Bibliography

Adorno, T.W., 1962, *Introduction to the Sociology of Music*, Trans. E.B. Ashton. New York.

African Position Paper and Draft Proposal for the Establishment of the African World Heritage Fund. (WHC-05/29.COM/11C2.Rev. Durban 10 July 2005).

Alpers, E. & Teelock, V., 2001, *History, Memory and Identity*, Bell Village, Port Louis: Nelson Mandela Center for African Culture.

Alpers, E., 2002, 'Imagining the Indian Ocean World', Opening Address to the International Conference on Cultural Exchange and Transformation in the Indian Ocean World. California: UCLA.

Arago, J., 1822, (Tome 1, 223-224), in Alpers, E. & Teelock, V., 2001, *History, Memory and Identity*, Bell Village, Port Louis: Nelson Mandela Center for African Culture.

Arendt, H., 1958, *The Human Condition*. Chicago: University of Chicago Press.

Asad, T., 1979, 'Anthropology and the Analysis of Ideology', *Man* 14: 603-27.

Askew, K., 2002, *Performing the Nation: Swahili Music and Cultural Politics in Tanzania*. Chicago: University of Chicago Press.

Arizpe, L., 2004, 'Intangible Cultural Heritage, Diversity and Coherence', *Museum International*, 56 (1/2): 103-7.

Bauman, Z., 1989, *Modernity and the Holocaust*, New York: Cornell University Press.

Barra, J., 1996, *Culture and Food*, Victoria, Seychelles: National Heritage Research Section (NHD).

Benoit, G., 1985, *The Afro-Mauritians: An Essay*, Reduit: Mahatma Gandhi Institute.

Challenges to the Management of Intangible Cultural Heritage

Berge, G., 1987, *Hierarchy, Equality and Social Change: Exchange Processes on a Seychelles Plantation*, No. 12, Occasional Papers in Social Anthropology, Department of Social Anthropology: Oslo, Norway.

Bernard, H. R., 1995, *Research Methods in Anthropology: Qualitative and Quantitative Approaches*. London: Sage.

Blacking, J., 1981, 'Making Artistic Popular Music: The Goal of True Folk', *Popular Music* 1: 9-25.

Blum, S., 1990, 'Commentary', *Ethnomusicology* 34: 413-21.

Boiles, C., 1982, 'Processes of Musical Semiosis', *Yearbook of Traditional Music* 14: 24-44.

Bouchenaki, M., 2003, 'The Interdependency of the Tangible and Intangible Cultural Heritage', The World Heritage Convention: Future Challenges and Possible Lines of Actions, European Conference, Røros, Norway, 3-5 September 2003.

Bourdieu, P., 1977, *Outline of a Theory of Practice*, Cambridge: Cambridge University Press.

Bourdieu, P., 1984, *Distinction: A Social Critique of the Judgment of Taste*, Cambridge: Cambridge University Press.

Bourdieu, P., 1996, *In Other Words*, Stanford: Stanford University Press.

Boswell, R., 2004, 'Cool politics: challenges to the management of intangible cultural heritage in Zanzibar', ISER Seminar, 21 September 2004. Rhodes University: Grahamstown.

Boswell, R., 2006, 'Say what you like: dress, identity and heritage in Zanzibar', *International Journal of Heritage Studies* 12(5), pp.440-57.

Boswell, R., 2005, 'Heritage tourism and identity in the Mauritian villages of Chamarel and Le Morne', *Journal of Southern African Studies*, 31 (2): 283-97.

Boswell, R., (forthcoming 2008), 'Scents of Identity: Intangible Cultural Heritage in Zanzibar' *Journal of Contemporary African Studies*.

Campbell, A. and Gibbs, J., 1986, *Violent transactions*, Oxford: Blackwell.

Chaudhuri, K. N., 1985, *Trade and Civilization in the Indian Ocean. An Economic History from the Rise of Islam to 1750*, Cambridge: Cambridge University Press.

Cohen, E., 1982, 'Marginal paradises: bungalow tourism on the islands of southern Thailand', *Annals of Tourism Research*, 9: 89-103.

Comaroff, J., 2001, 'Reflections on the colonial state, in South Africa and elsewhere: factions, fragments, facts and fictions', in *Social Identities in the New South Africa, After Apartheid – Volume One*, Zegeye, A., ed., Cape Town: Kwela Books.

Coser, L.A., 1956, *The Functions of Social Conflict*, London: Routledge & Kegan Paul.

Crick, M., 1989, 'Representations of international tourism in the social sciences: sun, sex, sights, savings and servility', *Annual Review of Anthropology*, 18: 307-44.

Didier, M., 1990, *Pages Africaines de l'Ile Maurice*, Bell Village, Port Louis: Nelson Mandela Centre for African Culture.

Edensor, T., 2000, 'Staging tourism, tourists as performers', *Annals of Tourism Research*, 27(2): 322-44.

Eriksen, T.H., 2001, 'Between universalism and relativism: a critique of the UNESCO concept of culture', in Cowan, J. K., Dembour, M-B. & Wilson, R. A., eds., *Culture and Rights: Anthropological Perspectives*, Cambridge: Cambridge University Press.

Eriksen, T.H., 2002, *Ethnicity and Nationalism*, (2nd Edition,), London: Pluto Press.

Essack, G., 1985, 'Lesperyans II A/10.12 Felix Joliecoeur', Victoria, Seychelles: NHD.

Fabian, J., 1983, *Time and the Other: How Anthropology Made Its Object*, New York

Fair, L., 2001, *Pastimes and Politics: Culture, Community and Identity in Post-Abolition Zanzibar*, Oxford: James Currey.

Fairweather, I., 2000, 'Without culture there is no future: The role of the heritage industry in post-Apartheid Southern Africa', (AASA conference 8-13 May 2000, Namibia).

Fanon, F., 1963, *The Wretched of the Earth*, New York: Grove.

Fekri, H., 2003, *Periodic Report on Africa 2002*, Paris: UNESCO.

Feld, S., 1974, 'Linguistic models in ethnomusicology', *Ethnomusicology* 18: 197-217.

Feld, S. & Fox, A. A., 1999, 'Music and language', *Annual Review of Anthropology*, 23: 25-53.

Feldman, A., 1991, *Formations of Violence: The narrative of the body and political terror in Northern Ireland*, Chicago/London: University of Chicago Press.

Finke, J., 2002, *The Rough Guide to Zanzibar*, London: Rough Guides Ltd.

Foucault, M., 1979, *Discipline and Punish*, New York: Vintage.

Garcìa-Canclini, N., 1995, *Hybrid Cultures: Strategies for Entering and Leaving Modernity*, Minneapolis: University of Minnesota Press.

Garrod, B. and Fyall, A., 2000, 'Managing heritage tourism', *Annals of Tourism Research* 27 (3): 682-708.

Geertz, C., 1973, *The Interpretation of Cultures*, New York.

Ghosh, R. N., Siddique, M. A. B. and Gabbay, R., 2003, *Tourism and Economic Development: Case Studies from the Indian Ocean Region*, Aldershot: Ashgate.

Gluckman, H. M., 1955, 'The peace in the feud', in Gluckman, H. M., *Custom and Conflict in Africa*, Oxford: Blackwell, chapter 1: 1-26.

Gluckman, H. M., 1963, *Order and rebellion in tribal Africa*, London: Cohen & West.

Goody, J., 2004, 'The transcription of oral heritage', *Museum International*, 56 (1/2): 91-97.

Grenier, L. & Guibault, J., 1990, 'Authority" revisited: The "Other" in anthropology and popular music studies', *Ethnomusicology* 34: 381-97.

Habermas, J., 1975, 'Towards a reconstruction of Historical Materialism', *Theory and Society*, 2: 287-300.

Hoerder, D., 2003, 'Transcultural states, nations and people', in *The Historical Practice of Diversity: Transcultural Interactions From the Early Modern Mediterranean to the Postcolonial World*, Hoerder, D., Harzig, C. and Shubert, A., eds., New York: Berghahn Books.

Hopkins, P., 1977, 'The homology of music and myth: views of Lévi-Strauss on musical structure', *Ethnomusicology* 21: 247-61.

Jiménex, A. C., 2003, 'Working out personhood: notes on "labour" and its anthropology', *Anthropology Today*, 19 (5): 14-17.

Keil, C., 1987, 'Participatory discrepancies and the power of music', *Cultural Anthropology*, 2: 275-83.

Kirshenblatt-Gimblett, B., 2004, 'Intangible heritage and the metacultural production of heritage', *Museum International*, 56 (1/2): 52-66.

Kleinman, A., 1997, *The Violences of Everyday Life: The Multiple Forms and Dynamics of Social Violence*.

Kurin, R., 2004, 'Safeguarding intangible cultural heritage in the 2003 UNESCO convention: a critical appraisal', *Museum International*, 56 (1/2): 66-78.

Le Chartier, C., 1993, *Ti-Frère Poète du Quotidien*, Bell Village, Port Louis: Centre Culturel Africain.

Levinas, E., 1986, 'Useless suffering', in *Face to Face with Levinas*, Richard Cohn, ed., State University of New York Press.

Lomax, A., 1968, *Folk Song Style and Culture*, Washington, DC.

Long, D. L., 1999, 'Cultural heritage management in post colonial polities: NOT the heritage of the Other', Symposium: *Theorising a Realm of Practice: Research Agendas in Archaeological Heritage Management*, World Archaeological Congress, University of Cape Town, 10-14 January 1999.

Lutz, W., 1994, *Population, Development, Environment: Understanding their Interactions in Mauritius*, Berlin: Springer-Verlag.

Martin, P. M., 1983, 'The violence of empire', in D. Birmingham & P.M. Martin, eds., *History of Central Africa*, London: Heinemann, pp. 1-26.

McPherson, K., 1984, 'Cultural Exchange in the Indian Ocean Region', *Westerly*, 29 (4): 5-16.

Merriam, A. P., 1964, *The Anthropology of Music*, Evanston.

Miles, W.F.S., 1999, "The Creole malaise in Mauritius", *African Affairs* 98(391): 211-29.

Moodie, T.D., 2005, 'Race and Ethnicity in South Africa' in Spickard, P. (ed) *Race and Nation: Ethnic Systems in a Modern World*. London: Routledge.

Munjeri, D., 2004, 'Tangible and intangible heritage: from difference to convergence', *Museum International*, 56 (1/2): 12-21.

Nagapen, A., 1998, *Le Marronage à Ille de France – Ile Maurice: Rêve ou riposte de l'Esclave?*, Port Louis: Centre Culturel Africain.

National Heritage Division (Seychelles), 2005, *Draft Research Agreement*, June 2005.

Nattiez, J-J., 1975, *Fondements D'une Sémiologie De La Musique*, Paris.

Ost, F., 2001, 'The heritage and future generations', *Keys to the 21st Century*, Paris: UNESCO.

Parkin, D., 2001, 'The commercialisation of biomedicine and the politics of flight in Zanzibar, Tanzania', in Cohen, R., ed., *Migration and Health in Southern Africa*, Cape Town: University of Cape Town Press, 150-62.

Pattullo, P., 1996, *Last Resorts: The Cost of Tourism in the Caribbean*, London: Cassell.

Partners for Africa Provisional Programme, 16 July 2005 (SAHRA).

Pearce, S. M., 1998, 'The construction of heritage: the domestic context and its implications', *International Journal of Heritage Studies*, 4 (2): 86-102.

Pearson, M., 1985, 'Littoral society: the case for the coast', *The Great Circle*, 7 (1):1-8.

Presentation of the World Heritage Fund Budget Proposed for the Biennium 2006-2007. (WHC-05/29.COM/16. Paris, 30 June 2005), Paris: UNESCO.

Progress Report on the Implementation of the Recommendation of the Periodic Report for Africa 2002-2005 and AFRICA 2009. (WHC-05/29.COM/11C. Paris 15 June 2005), Paris: UNESCO.

Radice, A., 2003, 'Has the past got any future?', *Contemporary Review*, 282 (1649): 370-2.

Remond-Gouillod, M., 2001, 'Evolving conceptions of heritage', *Keys to the 21st Century*, Paris: UNESCO.

Rice, T., 1986, 'Toward the remodelling of ethnomusicology', *Ethnomusicology*, 31: 469-88.

Riches, D., 1986, *The Anthropology of Violence*, Oxford: Blackwell.

Sala-Molins, L., 1987, *Le Code Noir our Le Calvaire de Canaan*, Paris: P.U.F. Pratiques Théoriques.

Scheper-Hughes, N., 1992, *Death without Weeping: The Violence of Everyday Life in Brazil*, Berkeley: University of California Press.

Scheper-Hughes, N., 1995, 'The primacy of the ethical, propositions for a militant anthropology', *Current Anthropology*, 36 (3).

Scheper-Hughes, N., 2001, 'The genocide continuum: peacetime crimes and the violence of everyday life', The 2001 Surjit Singh Lecture in Comparative Religious Thought and Culture. http://www.gtu.edu/lect_singh.php?singhid=13.

Sheriff, A., 1987, *Slaves, Spices and Ivory in Zanzibar*, London: James Currey.

Seeger, A., 1989, *Why Suya Sing: A Musical Ethnography of an Amazonian People*, Cambridge: Cambridge University Press.

St-Pierre, P., 12 March 2004, 'Le sécret de tangalé', *l'Express* p. 9.

Taussig, M., 1989, 'Terror as usual', *Social Text* (Fall-Winter): 3-20.

Teelock, V., 1998, *Bitter Sugar, Sugar and Slavery in 19th Century Mauritius*, Réduit: Mahatma Gandhi Institute.

Turnpenny, M., 2004, 'Cultural Heritage, an ill-defined concept? A call for joined-up policy', *International Journal of Heritage Studies* 10 (3): 295-307.

Ulin, R. C., 2002, 'Work as Cultural Production: labour and self-identity among southwest French wine-growers', *Journal of the Royal Anthropological Institute*, 8: 691-712.

Van Binsbergen, W. M. J., 1981, *Religious Change in Zambia: Exploratory studies*, London and Boston: Kegan Paul International.

Van Binsbergen, W. M. J., 2002, *Violence in Anthropology: Theoretical and Personal Remarks*, Leiden: Vrije Universiteit.

Van der Mescht, H. 2004. 'Phenomenology in Education: A Case Study in Education Leadership.' *Indo-Pacific Journal of Phenomenology* 4(1), pp. 1-16.

Van Zanten, W., 2004, 'Constructing new terminology for intangible cultural heritage', *Museum International*, 56 (1/2): 36-45.

Vere de Allen, J., 1980, 'A Proposal for Indian Ocean Studies', *Historical Relations Across the Indian Ocean, The General History of Africa*, Studies and Documents 3, Paris: UNESCO.

Wallis, R. & Malm, K., 1984, *Big Sounds from Small Peoples: The Music Industry in Small Countries*, London.

Wallis, R. & Malm, K., 1987, 'The International Music Industry and Transcultural Communication', in Lull, ed., 112-37.

Wendland, W., 2004, 'Intangible Heritage and Intellectual Property: challenges and future prospects', *Museum International*, 56 (1/2): 97-118.

Zegeye, A., 2001, *Social Identities in the New South Africa, After Apartheid – Volume One*, Cape Town: Kwela Books.

www.ingramcontent.com/pod-product-compliance
Lightning Source LLC
Chambersburg PA
CBHW021835300426
44114CB00009BA/448